THE 3-MINUTE

Reset

DEVOTIONAL
FOR WOMEN

THE 3-MINUTE

Reset

DEVOTIONAL
FOR WOMEN

365 Bible Readings to

Recharge Your Spirit

BARBOUR
PUBLISHING

© 2024 by Barbour Publishing, Inc.

ISBN 978-1-63609-807-4

Cover Design: Greg Jackson, Thinkpen Design

Published by Barbour Publishing, Inc., 1810 Barbour Drive, Uhrichsville, Ohio 44683, www.barbourbooks.com

Our mission is to inspire the world with the life-changing message of the Bible.

ecpa Member of the
Evangelical Christian
Publishers Association

Printed in China.

THE THINGS THAT ARE ABOVE

*If then you have been raised with Christ, seek the
things that are above, where Christ is, seated at the
right hand of God. Set your minds on things that
are above, not on things that are on earth.*
COLOSSIANS 3:1–2 ESV

If you believe in and have received Jesus Christ as your one
and only Savior from your sin, then you have been raised with
Christ and have every reason to celebrate! Our hope and healing
are in Christ. Our real life is in Christ. If we focus on the things
of earth, where everything will pass away, we have no hope,
no healing. Instead, we must lift our minds to focus on those
"things that are above" this temporary, broken world—where
Christ is seated at the right hand of God in the perfect forever
kingdom of heaven and where all who have been raised with
Christ truly belong.

*Dear Jesus, please help me keep my mind set far
above this hopeless, hurting world. All of my life,
all of my hope and healing, are in You alone. Amen.*

Day 2
SAY "YES"

For the Lord God is a sun and shield: the LORD
will give grace and glory: no good thing will he
withhold from them that walk uprightly.
PSALM 84:11 KJV

You have a Father who owns the cattle on a thousand hills and holds the cosmos in His hands. This Almighty Father generously offers all He has to you. He offers you a life overflowing with joy, comfort, and blessing. But like any gift, this one has to be accepted before it can be enjoyed. Today, why not say yes to the Father who loves you? Tell Him how you long to live—and love—like His cherished child.

Yes, Father! I choose to trust you in times of plenty
and in times when I have great need. I accept Your
life and peace; this is what fills my heart with joy,
comfort, and blessing even in the midst of difficulty.

Day 3

LONGING FOR HOME

This is what the LORD says: "You will be in Babylon for seventy years. But then I will come and do for you all the good things I have promised, and I will bring you home again."
JEREMIAH 29:10 NLT

Sometimes in life we go through periods when we feel out of place, as though we just don't belong. Our hearts feel restless and lonely. We long to go home, but we don't know how. God uses those times to teach us special things we need to know. But He never leaves us in exile. His grace always brings us home.

Father, when I am in a season of loneliness and restlessness, help me to trust You to lead me home. Thank You for Your grace that guides me. Amen.

Day 4

LIFTED UP

*But those who trust in the LORD will find new strength.
They will soar high on wings like eagles. They will run
and not grow weary. They will walk and not faint.*
ISAIAH 40:31 NLT

———————

Do you ever have days when you ask yourself, "How much further can I go? How much longer can I keep going like this?" On days like that, you long to give up. You wish you could just run away from the world and hide. Trust God's grace to give you the strength you need, even then. Let Him lift you up on eagles' wings.

Heavenly Father, I place my trust in You. Thank You for the promise that I will soar high on eagles' wings. Give me rest for my weariness and strength for the journey. Amen.

Day 5

HIS INSTRUMENT

*"The Spirit of the Lord is on me, because he has anointed
me to proclaim good news to the poor. He has sent me
to proclaim freedom for the prisoners and recovery
of sight for the blind, to set the oppressed free."*

Luke 4:18 niv

Just as the Holy Spirit wants you to be free, He also wants to
use you as His instrument to breathe freedom and hope into
the world. Be His instrument today. Tell people the truly good
news that God loves them. Do whatever you can to spread
freedom and vision and hope. Be a vehicle of the Spirit's grace.

*Lord, I long to be Your instrument. Give me the grace and
wisdom to spread Your message of good news and freedom
to the oppressed. Thank You for the hope You bring. Amen.*

Day 6

BE INTENTIONAL

*For you have died, and your life is hidden with Christ in God.
When Christ who is your life appears, then you also will appear
with him in glory. Put to death therefore what is earthly in you.*
Colossians 3:3–5 esv

How exactly do we focus on the things above when we are
planted here in such a broken world? Countless trials, temptations, distractions, hardships, and wounds pull our minds
away from God above—and His Word says we must put all
those things to death! We have to be intentional and willing
to work to keep our attention fixed where it should be, with a
life devoted to learning from and living for God—through the
study of His Word, through prayer, through devoted worship,
through service to others, and through active participation in
His Church for the fellowship we need with other believers.
We must remember our life here on earth is temporary and
ask God to show us His purposes and plans. We seek His guidance moment by moment and day by day, trusting that He is
working all things together for good for those who love Him
(Romans 8:28).

*Heavenly Father, please help me put to death
what is earthly in me. Help me to be intentional,
like You are, every moment to keep my mind focused
above—on You and Your perfect plans. Amen.*

Day 7

GOD'S ACCEPTANCE

The LORD hath heard my supplication;
the LORD will receive my prayer.
PSALM 6:9 KJV

People talk about "accepting" God into their lives. But it's God's acceptance of us that makes this possible. Because Jesus gave His life to pay the price for all the wrongs we've ever done, our perfect God can accept us wholeheartedly, even though we're far from perfect people. God not only accepts us but also accepts our imperfect prayers. We don't have to worry about saying just the right words. The "perfect" prayer is simply sharing what's on our hearts.

Thank You that I didn't have to get all cleaned up before I could come to You, Jesus. I trust You to do the work in me to make me more like You day by day.

Day 8

THE DETAILS

She is clothed with strength and dignity,
and she laughs without fear of the future.
PROVERBS 31:25 NLT

God wants to clothe us with His strength, His dignity. He wants us to be whole and competent, full of His grace. When we are, we can look at the future and laugh, knowing that God will take care of the details as we trust Him to be the foundation of our lives.

Father, thank You for clothing me with strength and dignity.
Thank You that I can look to my future without fear, confident
that You have all the details in Your hands. Amen.

PART OF THE BODY

Now you are the body of Christ and individually members of it. And God has appointed in the church first apostles, second prophets, third teachers, then miracles, then gifts of healing, helping, administrating, and various kinds of tongues.

1 CORINTHIANS 12:27–28 ESV

You became part of the body of Christ when you received Jesus as your Savior. Everyone who is saved is part of the body. And to have real hope and healing throughout all of your life, being an active part of a local fellowship of believers is crucial. Are you involved in a healthy local church where each member knows his or her unique gifts and uses them in collaboration to care for each other and to further God's kingdom? Read all of 1 Corinthians 12 and pray for God to lead you if you have not found that kind of church yet. And if you already have, pray regularly for God to protect and develop your church and help it continue to thrive.

Heavenly Father, thank You that I am part of Your body of believers. Please heal us, fill us continually with hope in You, and keep us healthy. Amen.

Day 10

LETTING GO

A peaceful heart leads to a healthy body;
jealousy is like cancer in the bones.
PROVERBS 14:30 NLT

Some emotions are meant to be nourished, and others need to be quickly dropped into God's hands. Learn to cultivate and seek out that which brings peace to your heart. And practice letting go of your negative feelings as quickly as you can, releasing them to God. If you cling to these dark feelings, they will reproduce like a cancer and block the healthy flow of grace into your life.

Oh God, search me and know my heart. Expose any negative feelings in me. Help me to leave them at the cross. Cleanse me and fill my heart with Your peace. Amen.

Day 11

DRAWING BACK THE CURTAINS

But whenever someone turns to the Lord, the veil is taken away. . . . So all of us who have had that veil removed can see and reflect the glory of the Lord. And the Lord—who is the Spirit—makes us more and more like him as we are changed into his glorious image.
2 Corinthians 3:16, 18 NLT

Sometimes we feel as though a thick, dark curtain hangs between us and God, hiding Him from our sight. But the Bible says that all we have to do is turn our hearts to the Lord and the curtain will be drawn back, letting God's glory and grace shine into our lives. When that happens, we can soak up the light, allowing it to renew our hearts and minds into the image of Christ.

Lord, thank You for removing the veil that hung between us. Turn my heart to You and draw me to Your light, renewing my heart and mind and making me more like Christ. Amen.

Day 12

FREE GIFT

*I have hated them that regard lying
vanities: but I trust in the LORD.*
PSALM 31:6 KJV

Religion is man-made, not God-made. Having a personal relationship with God is something totally different. It's not a list of rules and regulations or something we only "do" on Sundays. It's a love story between Father and child, a relationship in which we're totally accepted and unconditionally loved. Since we can't earn God's acceptance—it's a free gift of grace—that means we can't lose it either. God's acceptance releases us from the fear of rejection, so we're free to truly be ourselves.

I cannot fathom Your great gift, God. Thank You for bringing me freedom in Christ alone. Thank You for Your unfailing love for me. Show me how to love like that.

Day 13

ALL WHO TOUCHED HIM WERE HEALED

The people recognized Jesus at once, and they ran throughout the whole area, carrying sick people on mats to wherever they heard he was. Wherever he went—in villages, cities, or the countryside—they brought the sick out to the marketplaces. They begged him to let the sick touch at least the fringe of his robe, and all who touched him were healed.

MARK 6:54–56 NLT

How heartbreaking it must have been to see so many sick people in the villages and towns and rural areas where Jesus went. But how amazing to see Jesus heal them with even just a touch to the fringe of His robe! Imagine the awe and relief and rejoicing and celebration! Our minds can barely comprehend it. Though we don't have Jesus in the flesh with us today so we can witness His miraculous healing firsthand, we do have the Holy Spirit He sent to us. The same power of God in the Holy Spirit is able to heal and do anything God chooses.

Dear Jesus, I wish I could have seen You in person here on earth, but I trust in Your healing power. I trust that Your Holy Spirit is here now and is able to heal and do absolutely anything according to God's will. I pray that Your will be done in all things. Amen.

Day 14

RECIPROCAL

When we get together, I want to encourage you in your faith, but I also want to be encouraged by yours.

Encouragement is always reciprocal. When we encourage others, we are ourselves encouraged. In the world's economy, we pay a price in order to receive something we want; in other words, we give up something to get something. But in God's economy, we always get back what we give up. We are connected to each other, like parts of a body. Whatever good things we do for another are good for us as well.

God, thank You for the encouragement I find from my brothers and sisters in You. Help me to both share and receive the encouragement of Your love. Amen.

Day 15

THE PRESENT MOMENT

"This day is holy to our Lord."
NEHEMIAH 8:10 NIV

Sometimes we're in such a hurry to get to the future that we miss out on the present. God has gifts He wants to give you right now. Don't be so excited about tomorrow that you overlook the grace He's giving you today.

Heavenly Father, thank You for the gift of this moment. Keep my eyes and heart focused on the here and now, and immerse me in Your grace. Amen.

Day 16

JOY OF LIVING

Thou hast also given me the shield of thy salvation: and thy right hand hath holden me up, and thy gentleness hath made me great.

PSALM 18:35 KJV

Accomplishing something worthwhile is one of the joys of living. It can give you a sense of purpose and worth. But you are more than the sum of your accomplishments. You are an accomplished woman simply by continuing to mature into the individual God created you to be. Enjoy using every gift, talent, and ability God has so generously woven into you, while resting in the fact that you are worthy of God's love, regardless of what you've achieved.

I'm so thankful for the love and life You've poured into me. Your blessings and goodness allow me to bless others with what You've given me. Fill up my heart so that I may serve You and others with true joy.

Day 17

TAKE EVERY THOUGHT CAPTIVE

Though we live in the world, we do not wage war as the world does. The weapons we fight with are not the weapons of the world. On the contrary, they have divine power to demolish strongholds. We demolish arguments and every pretension that sets itself up against the knowledge of God, and we take captive every thought to make it obedient to Christ.

2 Corinthians 10:3–5 niv

Every trial, temptation, or distraction that hinders our hope and our healing can be demolished through the power of God working within us. Satan, our enemy, is always working in this world to spread his lies and destruction. But God is greater, and with His help we can capture each and every thought and argument that opposes Him and make it obedient to Christ. What does this look like in your life? What thoughts and arguments that oppose God's truth pester and plague you the most, and how are you capturing them and making them obedient to Christ?

Heavenly Father, please make me wise and discerning and powerful against the strongholds and lies of this world that the enemy uses to try to separate me from You. I want my every thought captivated by and focused on You! Amen.

Day 18

GRACE FOR EACH DAY

*May the Lord direct your hearts into God's
love and Christ's perseverance.*
2 THESSALONIANS 3:5 NIV

Allow God to lead you each day. His grace will lead you deeper
and deeper into the love of God—a love that heals your wounds
and works through you to touch those around you. Just as
Christ never gave up but let love lead Him all the way to the
cross, so too God will direct you all the way, giving you the
strength and the courage you need to face each challenge.

*Lord, direct my heart into Your love and into
the perseverance of Christ. Lead me, by Your
grace, into a deeper love for You. Amen.*

Day 19

DESIGNED FOR GREAT THINGS

*Except the L*ORD* build the house,*
they labour in vain that build it.
PSALM 127:1 KJV

We were designed to do great things hand in hand with a very great God. So why not invite God to be your coworker in every endeavor you undertake today? Call on Him throughout the day, anytime you need wisdom, peace, or perseverance. Allow God to infuse you with creativity, humility, and compassion—regardless of the size of the task at hand. Your hard work, guided by prayer and undergirded by the Spirit of a mighty God, can accomplish amazing things.

My Creator God, Your works are beyond my understanding—and yet You want to partner with me! I invite You in to do just that. Speak wisdom and creativity to me as I work today for Your glory.

STEADFAST SAVIOR

Jesus Christ is the same yesterday and today and forever.
HEBREWS 13:8 NIV

Loss of a loved one can create devastating feelings of hopelessness and despair and wounds so painful they feel like they will never fully heal. The changes in life resulting from the absence of that loved one are confusing and overwhelming. It's hard to know if anything will ever feel normal again; it's easy to feel anxious every moment, wondering who or what you might lose next. And so the truth that Jesus Christ is the same yesterday, today, and forever is your anchor—steady, strong, and sure. Yes, life is full of unpredictable loss in this broken world. But you can never lose your Savior or the assurance that He never changes and is preparing your heavenly home where you'll live forever in perfect paradise.

Dear Jesus, be my steady anchor. Help me to trust that, no matter what is changing around me or what loss or despair I'm suffering, You remain the same. You are my steadfast Savior. Amen.

Day 21

WALK CONFIDENTLY

*"But blessed are those who trust in the L*ORD *and have made the L*ORD *their hope and confidence."*
JEREMIAH 17:7 NLT

What gives you confidence? Is it your clothes. . .your money. . .your skills? These are all good things, but they are blessings from God, given to you through His grace. When your hopes (in other words, your expectations for the future) rest only in God, then you can walk confidently, knowing He will never disappoint you.

Lord, You are my hope and my confidence. I place all my expectations for the future in You, knowing that You will never disappoint me. Thank You for Your love. Amen.

Day 22

HE'S WAITING. . .

"The eyes of the LORD watch over those who do right, and his ears are open to their prayers."
1 PETER 3:12 NLT

You don't have to try to get God's attention. He is watching you right now. His ear is tuned to your voice. All you need to do is speak, and He will hear you. Receive the gift of grace He gives to you through prayer. Tell God your thoughts, your feelings, your hopes, your joys. He's waiting to listen to you.

Father, what a comfort it is to know You are watching over me and that Your ears are always open to my prayers. Thank You for the gift of Your presence. Amen.

SELF-IMAGE

I will praise thee; for I am fearfully and wonderfully made.
PSALM 139:14 KJV

You are a living, breathing reason for praise. God formed only one of you: unique in appearance, intricate in design, priceless beyond measure. You were fashioned with both love and forethought. When you look in the mirror, is this what you reflect upon? If not, it's time to retrain your brain. Use the mirror as a touchstone to praise. Ask God, "What do You see when You look at me?" Listen quietly as God's truth helps retool your self-image.

Father, please tell me the truth about myself. Who am I? What do You see? Remind me of the truth of who I am in Christ. Fill me with Your radiant love, and let my life praise You.

THE POWER OF GOD FOR SALVATION

For I am not ashamed of the gospel, for it is the power of God for salvation to everyone who believes.
ROMANS 1:16 ESV

When we suffer the loss of a loved one, we can rejoice even in the midst of our heartache if we know our loved one had received Jesus Christ as Savior. If we are not confident of that, we will experience deeper pain and sorrow. In either case, the loss can motivate us to share the gospel more boldly, more frequently, and more sincerely in hopes that more people will listen and repent and receive Christ as the one and only way, truth, and life—and secure their heavenly home for the future.

Heavenly Father, please help me to use the pain of losing a loved one to motivate me to share Your message of salvation and eternal life with more and more people who desperately need to hear it. Amen.

PERFECTION

*I don't mean to say that I have already achieved these things
or that I have already reached perfection. But I press on to
possess that perfection for which Christ Jesus first possessed me.*
PHILIPPIANS 3:12 NLT

We are called to be perfect. Nothing else is good enough for
God's people. That doesn't mean we have an inflated sense
of our own worth. And it doesn't mean we beat ourselves up
when we fall short of perfection. We know that in our own
strength we can never hope to achieve perfection—but with
God's grace, anything is possible.

*Jesus, when I am weary, give me the strength to keep
pressing forward toward perfection. I want, more than
anything, to be like You. Fill me with Your grace. Amen.*

Day 26

ANOTHER MOMENT LONGER

Wait patiently for the LORD. Be brave and courageous. Yes, wait patiently for the LORD.
PSALM 27:14 NLT

Patience is all about waiting things out. It's about holding on another moment longer. It means enduring hard times. As a younger person, you probably felt you couldn't possibly endure certain things, but the older you get, the more you realize that you can. If you just wait long enough, the tide always turns. Hold on. Your life will change. God's grace will rescue you.

Lord, help me to wait patiently for You. Help me to be brave and courageous. Remind me that the tide does always turn and that You will come through for me. Amen.

NOTHING MORE VALUABLE

Wisdom is more valuable than gold and crystal. It cannot be purchased with jewels mounted in fine gold.
JOB 28:17 NLT

Money can't buy you love—and it can't buy wisdom either. Wisdom is more precious than anything this world has to offer. In fact, some passages of the Old Testament seem to indicate that Wisdom is another name for Jesus. Just as Jesus is the way, the truth, and the life, He is also the one who gives us the vision to see God's world all around us. No other gift is more valuable than Jesus.

Jesus, the way, the truth, and the life, give me Your vision. Help me to see the world through Your eyes. Help me to place my relationship with You above all else. Amen.

WONDERFUL!

Commit your actions to the LORD, and your plans will succeed.
PROVERBS 16:3 NLT

Just because we want something to happen, it doesn't mean it will—no matter how hard we pray. We've all found that out (often to our sorrow!). But when we truly commit everything we do to God, praying only for His grace to be given free rein in our lives, then we will be surprised by what comes about. It may not be what we imagined—but it will be wonderful!

Father, Your Word tells me that Your ways are not my ways.
I pray that I would graciously commit all my plans to You,
armed with the promise that You will help them succeed. Amen.

Day 29

DISCOVER BEAUTY

Thy hands have made me and fashioned me: give me understanding, that I may learn thy commandments.
Psalm 119:73 kjv

God isn't concerned with appearances. The Bible tells us God looks at peoples' hearts instead of what's on the outside. Perhaps that's because appearances can be deceiving. A woman can be beautiful in the world's eyes while her heart nurtures pride, deceit, lust, greed, or a host of other unlovely traits. By learning to look at people the way God does, from the inside out, we may discover beauty in others—and in ourselves—that we've never noticed before.

Show me what You see when You look at my heart, Lord. I pray You would fill my insides with the beauty that comes from knowing You. Help me always look for that beauty in those around me.

THE BIRDS WILL REMIND YOU

"Are not two sparrows sold for a penny? And not one of them will fall to the ground apart from your Father. But even the hairs of your head are all numbered. Fear not, therefore; you are of more value than many sparrows."
MATTHEW 10:29–31 ESV

Do you have favorite birds you watch for or whose songs you love to hear? Every time you see or hear God's avian creatures, think of this scripture and let it remind you how much you are loved and valued by your heavenly Father. If God knows and even cares about every sparrow, He surely knows and cares about you—so much so that He sent His Son to die to save you. He knows you so well that He has even counted the hairs on your head. He is good and sovereign over your life. Place all your hope in Him—there's no better place it could be!

Heavenly Father, I can't even begin to understand how You know everything about everything and everything about me too. But I am so grateful for Your love and care and salvation through Jesus. Amen.

ALL ALONE

*"But when you pray, go away by yourself, shut the
door behind you, and pray to your Father in private.
Then your Father, who sees everything, will reward you."*
MATTHEW 6:6 NLT

Prayer takes many shapes and forms. There's the corporate
kind of prayer, in which we open our hearts to God as part
of a congregation. There is also the kind of prayer that is said
quickly and on the run. But we need to make at least some time
in our lives for prayer in the privacy of a quiet place, where
we meet God's grace all alone.

*Lord, how I need You. Every moment of every day, I need
Your presence. Gently lead me into Your loving arms,
to set aside precious, quiet time with You. Amen.*

Day 32

OVERFLOWING LOVE

And may the Lord make your love for one another and for all
people grow and overflow, just as our love for you overflows.
1 THESSALONIANS 3:12 NLT

As a very young child, you thought you were the center of the world. As you grew older, you had to go through the painful process of learning that others' feelings were as important as yours. However, God's grace wants to lift your perspective even higher. He wants you to overflow with love for other people.

Lord, fill my heart with love for others. As I learn
to love You more and receive Your love, may my
love for Your children overflow. Amen.

Day 33

HEALING IN HIS WINGS

The LORD of Heaven's Armies says, "The day of judgment is coming, burning like a furnace. On that day the arrogant and the wicked will be burned up like straw. They will be consumed—roots, branches, and all. But for you who fear my name, the Sun of Righteousness will rise with healing in his wings. And you will go free, leaping with joy like calves let out to pasture."
MALACHI 4:1–2 NLT

Sometimes we think we can't heal from emotional pain until we get justice for wrongdoing against us. But we may never actually see that justice delivered in this life. Whether we do or not, we must heed the apostle Paul's words in the book of Romans where he admonishes, "Dear friends, never take revenge. Leave that to the righteous anger of God. For the Scriptures say, 'I will take revenge; I will pay them back,' says the LORD" (Romans 12:19 NLT). God sees and knows any wrongdoing against you. Let His righteous anger take care of it. Trust His perfect justice, and believe that He will heal you.

Heavenly Father, I need Your wisdom and self-control when I think about how I want justice for wrongdoing against me. I am trusting that You alone will deliver perfect justice. I give my anger and pain to You. Please replace them with peace and healing. Amen.

A LIVING BODY THAT LASTS FOREVER

Our body is like a house we live in here on earth. When it is destroyed, we know that God has another body for us in heaven. . . . This body will last forever. Right now we cry inside ourselves because we wish we could have our new body which we will have in heaven. We will not be without a body. We will live in a new body. While we are in this body, we cry inside ourselves because things are hard for us. It is not that we want to die. Instead, we want to live in our new bodies. We want this dying body to be changed into a living body that lasts forever. It is God Who has made us ready for this change. He has given us His Spirit to show us what He has for us.

2 CORINTHIANS 5:1–5 NLV

There's no stopping the aging process, no hope for immortality in these earthly bodies. But we have certain and secure hope because of Jesus that God is preparing new bodies for us in heaven that will be forever young. And while at times we do cry inside ourselves as we experience the brokenness of this world, we always have the Holy Spirit within us to encourage us and remind us of God's promises and truth.

Heavenly Father, I'm eager for my heavenly body and home that will last forever, but I'm also grateful for each day You give me on this earth. Please help me to persevere even when times are tough. Help me to do all the good things You have planned for me—until one day I become the new flawless me at home forever with You in heaven. Amen.

TRUSTWORTHY AND TRUE

Then I saw "a new heaven and a new earth," for the first heaven and the first earth had passed away, and there was no longer any sea. I saw the Holy City, the new Jerusalem, coming down out of heaven from God, prepared as a bride beautifully dressed for her husband. And I heard a loud voice from the throne saying, "Look! God's dwelling place is now among the people, and he will dwell with them. They will be his people, and God himself will be with them and be their God. 'He will wipe every tear from their eyes. There will be no more death' or mourning or crying or pain, for the old order of things has passed away." He who was seated on the throne said, "I am making everything new!" Then he said, "Write this down, for these words are trustworthy and true."

REVELATION 21:1–5 NIV

These words from Jesus are not just an empty or uncertain hope. They are solid and sure, "trustworthy and true." They are the ultimate, guaranteed reward of those who humbly put their trust in Jesus Christ as their one and only Savior from sin. Our perfect dwelling place with God, with no more sorrow or pain, is not *if* but *when*. Hallelujah!

Jesus my Savior, I expectantly and eagerly await that wonderful day when You make all things new. Until then, help me to live my life loving and serving You. Amen.

ACT AS TRUE CHILDREN OF GOD

*"Love your enemies! Pray for those who persecute you!
In that way, you will be acting as true children of your
Father in heaven. For he gives his sunlight to both the evil
and the good, and he sends rain on the just and the unjust
alike. If you love only those who love you, what reward is
there for that? Even corrupt tax collectors do that much.
If you are kind only to your friends, how are you different
from anyone else? Even pagans do that. But you are to
be perfect, even as your Father in heaven is perfect."*
MATTHEW 5:44–48 NLT

Whether we see justice for wrongdoing against us or not, God
calls us to love our enemies and pray for those who persecute
us. That instruction might seem absolutely upside-down crazy
and impossible, but Jesus would not have taught it if it were
not good for us. When we love our enemies and pray for those
who persecute us, we draw closer to our heavenly Father and
become more like Him. The closer we are to Him and the more
we act like Him, the more we experience hope and healing.

*Dear Jesus, through Your great power, please help
me to do what seems impossible—help me to love my
enemies and pray for those who persecute me. Amen.*

Day 37

HOPE FOR OUR DREAM HOME

*How beautiful are the places where You live, O Lord of all!
My soul wants and even becomes weak from wanting to
be in the house of the Lord. . . . How happy are those who
live in Your house! They are always giving thanks to You.*
PSALM 84:1–2, 4 NLV

Do you ever think about and hope for a dream house? What
would it look like, and where would it be located? It's fun to
imagine! But better than any home we can dream up here on
earth is the forever home God is creating for us in heaven.
And when we take time to focus on God and praise Him and
hear from Him through His Word, we get little glimpses of how
incredible that perfect forever home will be!

*Heavenly Father, thank You for my blessings here and now
where I live on earth. Even more, thank You for the perfect home
with You that You are making in heaven for me forever! Amen.*

Day 38

ONLY BY GRACE

*Accept one another, then, just as Christ accepted
you, in order to bring praise to God.*
ROMANS 15:7 NIV

It's easy to pick out others' faults. Sometimes you may even
feel justified in doing so, as though God will approve of
your righteousness as you point out others' sinfulness. Don't
forget that Christ accepted you with all your brokenness
and faults. Only by grace were you made whole. Share that
grace—that acceptance and unconditional love—with the people
around you.

*Jesus, what a joy it is to know that You have
accepted me just as I am! You have made me whole.
Help me to pass that grace on to others. Amen.*

Day 39

NO GREATER ASSURANCE

*The Lord will perfect that which concerneth
me: thy mercy, O Lord, endureth for ever.*
Psalm 138:8 kjv

Throughout scripture, God continually reassures us that He's working on our behalf to accomplish the good things He has planned for our lives. If your confidence wavers, if you need to know for certain someone is on your side, if you're anxious about the future, do what people who've felt the very same way have done for centuries: take God's words to heart. There's no greater assurance than knowing you're loved, completely and eternally.

*Father, I bring all my thoughts and feelings to You at this
moment. Take my worries, and speak truth into my life.
Remind me that You are here and at work in my life.*

Day 40

THE GREATNESS OF HIS LOVE

Christ will make his home in your hearts as you trust in him. Your roots will grow down into God's love and keep you strong. And may you have the power to understand, as all God's people should, how wide, how long, how high, and how deep his love is. May you experience the love of Christ, though it is too great to understand fully. Then you will be made complete with all the fullness of life and power that comes from God. Now all glory to God, who is able, through his mighty power at work within us, to accomplish infinitely more than we might ask or think.

EPHESIANS 3:17–20 NLT

Sometimes we feel hopeless because we fail to realize and focus on God's amazing love for us. If we could fully understand the breadth and length and height and depth of His love, we would never worry or feel scared or hopeless about a thing ever again. Think on Jesus' sacrifice to save you from sin. Think on all the other many blessings in your life. Trust that God will continue to care for you. He is able to do so much more than you could ever dream.

Dear Jesus, help me to realize and focus on Your incredible love more and more each day. Amen.

OUR BLESSED HOPE

*For the grace of God has appeared, bringing salvation
for all people, training us to renounce ungodliness and
worldly passions, and to live self-controlled, upright,
and godly lives in the present age, waiting for our blessed
hope, the appearing of the glory of our great God and
Savior Jesus Christ, who gave himself for us to redeem us
from all lawlessness and to purify for himself a people for
his own possession who are zealous for good works.*

TITUS 2:11–14 ESV

Our blessed hope is the appearing of Jesus. We are always to
be watching for His return. He promises He will, and it will
be unlike anything any person has ever experienced. But it
will be wonderful for everyone who loves and trusts in Him
as Savior. Mark 13:24–27 (NLT) says: "At that time, after the
anguish of those days, the sun will be darkened, the moon will
give no light, the stars will fall from the sky, and the powers in
the heavens will be shaken. Then everyone will see the Son of
Man coming on the clouds with great power and glory. And he
will send out his angels to gather his chosen ones from all over
the world—from the farthest ends of the earth and heaven."

*Dear Jesus, You are my blessed hope! I'm watching
and waiting for You to return and gather Your people—
including me! I love You and trust You! Amen.*

Day 42

FIX YOUR EYES ON JESUS

Therefore, since we are surrounded by such a great cloud of witnesses, let us throw off everything that hinders and the sin that so easily entangles. And let us run with perseverance the race marked out for us, fixing our eyes on Jesus, the pioneer and perfecter of faith. For the joy set before him he endured the cross, scorning its shame, and sat down at the right hand of the throne of God. Consider him who endured such opposition from sinners, so that you will not grow weary and lose heart.
Hebrews 12:1–3 niv

Sometimes we allow things into our lives that drain us and hinder us and make us lose focus on the great hope we have in Jesus. Can you take time to evaluate what's weighing you down and, especially, repent of any sin you are holding on to? Like the psalmist, pray: "Create in me a pure heart, O God, and renew a steadfast spirit within me" (Psalm 51:10 niv). Then fix your eyes on Jesus and keep running with perseverance the race God has set for you, doing all the good things He has planned for you along the way.

Dear Lord, please help me to rid my life of anything that takes my focus off You. My life is in You and for You, and I want to run well this race You have set for me until I'm with You at the finish line. Amen.

NO ONE HAS TO CRUMBLE

"Why do you call me 'Lord, Lord,' and not do what I tell you? Everyone who comes to me and hears my words and does them, I will show you what he is like: he is like a man building a house, who dug deep and laid the foundation on the rock. And when a flood arose, the stream broke against that house and could not shake it, because it had been well built. But the one who hears and does not do them is like a man who built a house on the ground without a foundation. When the stream broke against it, immediately it fell, and the ruin of that house was great."

LUKE 6:46–49 ESV

Those who call Jesus "Lord" but don't actually do what He says are in danger of hopelessly caving and crumbling through life's hardship and pain. But no one has to live that way! Those who call Jesus "Lord" and actually listen and obey and have a relationship with Him—it's like they're building their lives on solid rock. When the rains and storms and floods of life come, those whose foundation is built on Jesus don't need to worry about crumbling and washing away. They will stand strong through anything because they stand on Jesus.

Dear Jesus, I want my life to be rock solid and strong because my foundation is obedience to You! Teach and build me through Your Holy Word. Amen.

Day 44

NEW STRENGTH

"In quietness and confidence is your strength."
Isaiah 30:15 nlt

The weaker we feel, the more we fret. The more we fret, the weaker we feel. It's a vicious circle. Stop the circle! Find a quiet place, if only for a few moments, to draw close to God. Grace will come to you through the quiet, and you will discover new strength.

Father, I desperately need You. Step in and take me out of the vicious circle of worry and fretting. Give me Your peace. Thank You for Your strength. Amen.

THE TONGUE OF THE WISE BRINGS HEALING

The words of the reckless pierce like swords,
but the tongue of the wise brings healing.
PROVERBS 12:18 NIV

When you find yourself suffering from an emotional wound, to whom do you go for a listening ear, to talk out the pain and seek help and healing? It's easy to want to vent to anyone who will listen, but be careful. Scripture is clear you should not go to those who are reckless with their words, for they might only pierce your wound and injure you more. Instead, be intentional to seek out people who are wise, because their tongues will bring healing. Do you have those wise people in your life? If not, pray for God's direction toward and connection with wise people who love Him and His Word, who will give you both compassion and good counsel in any hard situation.

Heavenly Father, help me to be careful whom I vent to when I am emotionally wounded and hurting. Please guide me to wise people who can truly help me to heal. Amen.

Day 46

HOW MUCH CAN WE GIVE?

*Command those who are rich in this present world not to
be arrogant nor to put their hope in wealth, which is so
uncertain, but to put their hope in God, who richly provides
us with everything for our enjoyment. Command them
to do good, to be rich in good deeds, and to be generous
and willing to share. In this way they will lay up treasure
for themselves as a firm foundation for the coming age,
so that they may take hold of the life that is truly life.*

1 TIMOTHY 6:17–19 NIV

Our hopes and goals here on earth should never be about how much we can get. Rather, they should be about how much we can give, how many good works we can do to encourage others for God's glory and to point others to salvation in Jesus Christ. We are called to be generous givers with our money and our blessings, which ultimately come from God. His Word tells us to be ready to share and give and help others in need—and promises that we will gather up forever treasure in heaven by doing so. Money and the blessings of this world are only temporary, but the good and giving kinds of things we have done here on earth will matter in heaven for all eternity.

*Heavenly Father, help me to make goals based on how much
I can give, not how much I can get. I hope and trust in Your
promises about blessings and treasures in heaven. Amen.*

ALONE TIME WITH GOD

But Jesus often withdrew to the wilderness for prayer.
LUKE 5:16 NLT

God is always with us, even when we're too busy to do more than whisper a prayer in the shower or as we drive the car. But if even Jesus needed to make time to get away by Himself for some alone time with God, then we certainly need to do so too. In those quiet moments of prayer, by ourselves with God, we will find the grace we need to live our busy lives.

Jesus, thank You for Your constant presence with me.
Help me to make time with You a priority, knowing that putting
You first will make everything else fall into place. Amen.

Day 48

FOREVERMORE

The LORD shall preserve thy going out and thy coming in from this time forth, and even for evermore.
PSALM 121:8 KJV

Conventional wisdom tells us that nothing lasts forever. Thankfully, just because a saying is often quoted doesn't make it true. The time-tested wisdom of the Bible assures us that God always has been and always will be. Because of Jesus, forever is a word that can apply to us as well. When we follow Jesus here on earth, we follow Him straight to heaven. We have the assurance of knowing our true life span is "forevermore."

Jesus, thank You for the amazing truth that eternal life starts here and now. I don't have to wait for heaven to live the abundant life You have for me. "Your kingdom come" in my life and my actions today.

Day 49

WORDS LIKE HONEY

The heart of the wise has power over his mouth and adds learning to his lips. Pleasing words are like honey. They are sweet to the soul and healing to the bones.
PROVERBS 16:23–24 NLV

What you say and what others say to you will make a difference in your ability to heal from emotional wounds. If you only think and speak and hear negativity and bitterness, you will wallow endlessly in negativity and bitterness. You absolutely need the right times and places to let loose the reality of your pain in healthy ways, but with God's help and wisdom, you can maintain good self-control and keep learning and growing through your situation. Seek out words from others—and seek to use words yourself—that are pleasing like honey, that bring sweetness to your soul and healing to your bones.

Heavenly Father, help me to remove the thoughts and words from my mind and lips that make me wallow in pain. Fill me up with pleasing words to think and speak. Focus my attention on Your goodness and love to me, and please heal my wounds and heartache. Amen.

HOPE IN THE REAL DEAL

*Our God is in the heavens. He does whatever He wants to do.
Their gods are silver and gold, the work of human hands.
They have mouths but they cannot speak. They have eyes
but they cannot see. They have ears but they cannot hear.
They have noses but they cannot smell. They have hands
but they cannot feel. They have feet but they cannot walk.
They cannot make a sound come out of their mouths.
Those who make them and trust them will be like them.*

PSALM 115:3–8 NLV

This psalm compares our one true God with the fake gods of
the world that some people make for themselves. It describes
how ridiculous those fake gods are—they have useless mouths,
eyes, ears, noses, hands, and feet. But people often make fake
gods because they don't really want to serve or worship anyone
but themselves. And so they will end up as useless and mean-
ingless as those fake gods. But to trust and obey and worship
our extraordinary God, who is the real deal, is to live the life
you were created for, with love and hope and peace forever.

*One true God, I'm so thankful I hope and trust
in You, not a fake god. Help me to keep living for
You and sharing You with others. Amen.*

WATCH THE SKY

A cloud carried Him away so they could not see Him. They were still looking up to heaven, watching Him go. All at once two men dressed in white stood beside them. They said, "You men of the country of Galilee, why do you stand looking up into heaven? This same Jesus Who was taken from you into heaven will return in the same way you saw Him go up into heaven."
ACTS 1:9–11 NLV

After Jesus died and rose again, He remained on earth for forty days to prove Himself alive and teach His followers some more before going up to heaven in a cloud. His friends kept watching the sky, but then two angels appeared and said, "What are you doing? He'll come back again someday." It was time for His followers to get busy sharing about Jesus. Do you ever wish Jesus would hurry back and appear in the sky again? It will be amazing! But while we wait, we need to keep busy sharing the hope of the good news that Jesus died to save us from our sin and that He is alive now and will take all who trust in Him to heaven someday!

Dear Jesus, I'm watching the sky for You, but I'll also keep busy sharing Your good news! Amen.

RENEWAL

"Look, the winter is past, and the rains are over and gone."
SONG OF SOLOMON 2:11 NLT

Dreary times of cold and rain come to us all. Just as the earth needs those times to renew itself, so do we. As painful as those times are, grace works through them to make us into the people God has called us to be. But once those times are over, there's no need to continue to dwell on them. Go outside and enjoy the sunshine!

Father, it's easy to become discouraged during the long days of winter. But I know times of darkness are necessary to fully appreciate the joy of light. Help me to revel in Your sunlight. Amen.

ATTITUDE ADJUSTMENT

This is the day which the LORD hath made;
we will rejoice and be glad in it.
PSALM 118:24 KJV

What kind of day will you have today? Your answer might be, "I won't know until I've lived it!" But the attitude with which you approach each new day can change the way you experience life. That's why it's important to set aside some "attitude adjustment time" every morning. When you wake, remind yourself that "this is the day the Lord has made." Look for His hand in the details and thank Him for every blessing He brings your way.

I am Yours, and You are mine, Jesus! I go into this day with this truth in the forefront of my mind. Have Your way in me, Lord!

HE TOOK JESUS AT HIS WORD

*Once more he visited Cana in Galilee, where he had turned
the water into wine. And there was a certain royal official
whose son lay sick at Capernaum. When this man heard that
Jesus had arrived in Galilee from Judea, he went to him and
begged him to come and heal his son, who was close to death.*
JOHN 4:46–47 NIV

The desperation and the fear in this dad are hard to understand unless one has been in his shoes, having lost or nearly lost a child. He was a royal official but not too important or prideful to beg Jesus for help. And when Jesus said only the words, "Go, your son will live," the royal official stopped begging for Jesus to come to his son. He "took Jesus at his word and departed" (John 4:50 NIV). We too can take Jesus at His Word, sight unseen. Those of us who trust in Him as Savior are promised healing and eternal life. Sometimes miracles of healing are God's will in this earthly life; ultimately, they are His will for believers forevermore in heaven.

*Dear Jesus, even while desperate for the healing of
his son, the royal official took You at Your word and
trusted You completely—believed You had done the
healing—even before he saw the proof with his own
eyes. I want to have such great faith too. Amen.*

NO NEED TO WORRY

"Therefore I tell you, do not be anxious about your life, what you will eat or what you will drink, nor about your body, what you will put on. Is not life more than food, and the body more than clothing? Look at the birds of the air: they neither sow nor reap nor gather into barns, and yet your heavenly Father feeds them. Are you not of more value than they? And which of you by being anxious can add a single hour to his span of life?"
MATTHEW 6:25–27 ESV

When you trust God, you will always have what you need. He is your perfect provider! If you're ever fretting about finances or work or food or clothes or anything at all, come again to this scripture in Matthew 6. Read and believe that God takes good care of even the birds of the air—surely He takes even better care of you!

Heavenly Father, I don't want to be anxious about anything. Please take these worries of life from me. Remind me how You always provide for my every need. I hope and trust in You. Amen.

Day 56

WHAT YOU NEED

Give me neither poverty nor riches!
Give me just enough to satisfy my needs.
PROVERBS 30:8 NLT

———

God gives us what we need, and He knows exactly what and how much that is. Whatever He has given you financially, He knows that is what you need right now. Trust His grace. He will satisfy your needs.

Father, my provider, I thank You for giving me exactly what I need. Help me to trust You with Your provision for me and to know that Your grace is always enough for me. Amen.

Day 57

THE DEPTH OF GOD'S RICHES

*Oh, the depth of the riches of the wisdom and
knowledge of God! How unsearchable his
judgments, and his paths beyond tracing out!*
ROMANS 11:33 NIV

Money is the way our culture measures value, but we forget that it's just a symbol, a unit of measurement that can never span the infinite value of God's grace. Imagine trying to use a tape measure to stretch across the galaxy or a teaspoon to determine how much water is in the sea. In the same way, money will always fall short if we use it to try to understand the depth of God's riches.

Oh Father, there is no way I could begin to comprehend Your greatness. Your wisdom and knowledge would cause the oceans to overflow. Thank You for sharing Your wealth with me. Amen.

Day 58

TRULY TRUSTWORTHY

God is not man, that he should lie, or a son of man,
that he should change his mind. Has he said, and will he
not do it? Or has he spoken, and will he not fulfill it?
NUMBERS 23:19 ESV

If you have been lied to, let down, and betrayed too many times, you may have little to no hope of ever fully trusting any person again. When that fear of trusting threatens to send you spiraling into despair, instead let it urge you to cling harder to the one always worthy of every bit of your trust. He "has given both his promise and his oath. These two things are unchangeable because it is impossible for God to lie. Therefore, we who have fled to him for refuge can have great confidence as we hold to the hope that lies before us. This hope is a strong and trustworthy anchor for our souls" (Hebrews 6:18–19 NLT).

Heavenly Father, please heal my wounds from when I've been lied to, let down, and betrayed. Help me to cling to You most of all as my one true God, worthy of all my trust. And please lead me to the people who are filled with Your Spirit who will befriend and love me in good and honest ways. Amen.

THE LORD STANDS WITH YOU

The first time I was brought before the judge, no one came with me. Everyone abandoned me. May it not be counted against them. But the Lord stood with me and gave me strength so that I might preach the Good News in its entirety for all the Gentiles to hear. And he rescued me from certain death. Yes, and the Lord will deliver me from every evil attack and will bring me safely into his heavenly Kingdom.

2 TIMOTHY 4:16–18 NLT

Have you experienced, like Paul in this scripture, a time when everyone you knew abandoned you? Yet Paul didn't want to hold it against his friends because, even with no one else there to help, God Himself was with Paul and protected him and gave him power. How have you seen God help you like that? Paul trusted that God would keep away every evil plan that anyone might have against him. Do you trust that too? Paul also knew that someday God would bring him into heaven forever. And God promises that for you as well!

Heavenly Father, I trust that no matter what happens here in this world, ultimately You will always keep me safe because someday You are going to bring me into perfect paradise in heaven with You! Amen.

Day 60

SURRENDER

*"For whoever wants to save their life will lose it,
but whoever loses their life for me will save it."*

LUKE 9:24 NIV

Life is full of paradoxes. God seems to delight in turning our
ideas inside out and backward. It doesn't seem to make sense,
but the only way to possess our life is to surrender it absolutely
into God's hands. As we let go of everything, God's grace gives
everything back to us, transformed by His love.

*God, even when Your Word doesn't completely make sense,
help me to trust You implicitly. Give me the strength
to surrender every part of my life to You. Amen.*

WORD PICTURES

The LORD is my strength and my shield;
my heart trusted in him, and I am helped.
PSALM 28:7 KJV

A rock, a fortress, a warrior, a king—the Bible uses many metaphors to describe God. Since no single word can wholly describe our infinite, incomparable God, word pictures help us better connect a God we cannot see with images that we can. If your attitude could use a boost of strength and confidence, picture God as your shield. He is always there to protect you, to shelter you, and to guard your heart and mind.

Creator God, please use the imagination You gave
me to fill me with truths from Your Word. I lay my
thoughts at Your feet for You to transform.

DON'T BE DISMAYED

"So do not fear, for I am with you; do not be dismayed,
for I am your God. I will strengthen you and help you;
I will uphold you with my righteous right hand."
ISAIAH 41:10 NIV

No matter what you are going through, you have hope in any and every situation because God is your God. He never leaves you. Think of a time in your past when you were positive you would not survive the pain or hardship. How did you make it through? God never left you. What ways and what people did He provide to rescue you? He was continually strengthening and helping you, always holding you up with His righteous right hand. When you remember and thank Him and praise Him for specific ways He has helped you in the past, you gain confident hope and trust that He will do so again—right now and in the future.

Heavenly Father, You alone are my God. You have never left me and You never will. In the past, present, and future, I trust that You strengthen and help me and hold me up. Amen.

AMAZING LOVE

Your unfailing love, O LORD, is as vast as the heavens;
your faithfulness reaches beyond the clouds.
PSALM 36:5 NLT

God loves you. The Creator of the universe cares about you, and His love is unconditional and limitless. You can never make Him tired of you; He will never abandon you. You are utterly and completely loved, no matter what, forever and ever. Isn't that amazing?

Oh Father, I am so grateful for Your unfailing love, vast as the heavens, reaching beyond the clouds. Thank You for never abandoning me and for Your amazing grace. Amen.

A PLACE PREPARED FOR YOU

"Let not your hearts be troubled. Believe in God; believe also in me. In my Father's house are many rooms. If it were not so, would I have told you that I go to prepare a place for you? And if I go and prepare a place for you, I will come again and will take you to myself, that where I am you may be also. And you know the way to where I am going."

JOHN 14:1–4 ESV

Jesus is preparing a home for us in heaven, but like Thomas, sometimes we might wonder if we know exactly how to get there (John 14:5). Jesus answered him, "I am the way, and the truth, and the life. No one comes to the Father except through me" (John 14:6 ESV). And so we get there by following Jesus throughout this earthly life until one day we are in forever life in the home He has prepared for us in heaven. How do we follow Him? By reading His Word, living our lives humbly surrendered to His will, and trusting that we are guided by the Holy Spirit.

Dear Jesus, remind me every moment that You are the one and only way, truth, and life through this world. I will keep following You until the day I come home to be with You in perfect paradise forever. I'm so excited for that day! Amen.

Day 65

RADIANT

*"If you are filled with light, with no dark corners,
then your whole life will be radiant, as though
a floodlight were filling you with light."*
LUKE 11:36 NLT

We all have dark corners in our lives we keep hidden. We hide them from others. We hide them from God. And we even try to hide them from ourselves. But God wants to shine His light even into our darkest, most private nooks and crannies. He wants us to step out into the floodlight of His love—and then His grace will make us shine.

*Heavenly Father, fill me with light. Shine Your radiance
on all my dark corners. Remove my shame, and help
me to bask in the light of Your love. Amen.*

Day 66

THE ENTIRE PACKAGE

*He makes the whole body fit together perfectly. As each part
does its own special work, it helps the other parts grow,
so that the whole body is healthy and growing and full of love.*
Ephesians 4:16 nlt

God has a holistic perspective on health. He sees your body,
soul, heart, and mind, and He wants each part of you to be
strong and fit. He looks at our world in the same way, longing
to heal the entire package—society, the environment, and
governments. He wants His body on earth, the church, to be
whole and strong as well. Health pours out of Him, a daily
stream of grace on which we can rely for each aspect of life.

*Lord, I am grateful that You have enabled me to
be a part of Your body—the Church. Help me to
do my part so that all of us can grow. Amen.*

CONNECTION, COMFORT, AND CARE

*Ruth replied, "Don't urge me to leave you or to turn
back from you. Where you go I will go, and where
you stay I will stay. Your people will be my people and
your God my God. Where you die I will die, and there
I will be buried. May the LORD deal with me, be it ever
so severely, if even death separates you and me."*
RUTH 1:16–17 NIV

To heal from the pain and grief caused by the loss of a loved
one, we need to connect and cling to other good and loving relationships. Ruth's loyalty to Naomi after they had both suffered
loss is a beautiful example of how God healed and blessed them
both as they depended on each other and ultimately on God
in the midst of their grief and great need. Our enemy, Satan,
wants to isolate us when we are in pain so that he can wound
us even more and try to completely destroy us. So we must be
intentional to connect with others and let God's healing and
protection and blessing flow to us through the comfort and
care of those loving people He has placed in our lives.

*Heavenly Father, show me Your great love and healing
through the people You have placed in my life. Help me
to connect well with others so I can receive the comfort
and care You want to give me through them. Amen.*

Day 68

WITNESS OF LAUGHTER

We were filled with laughter, and we sang for joy. And the other nations said, "What amazing things the LORD has done for them."

PSALM 126:2 NLT

Life is truly amazing. Each day, grace touches us in many ways: from the sun on our faces to each person we meet, from the love of our friends and families to the satisfaction of our work. Pay attention. Let people hear you laugh more. Don't hide your joy. It's a witness to God's love.

Father, thank You for this amazing life and for Your grace that touches me in so many ways. Help me to wear my joy for all to see. Amen.

Day 69

NEVER GIVE UP

One day Jesus told his disciples a story to show that they should always pray and never give up. "There was a judge in a certain city," he said, "who neither feared God nor cared about people. A widow of that city came to him repeatedly, saying, 'Give me justice in this dispute with my enemy.' The judge ignored her for a while, but finally he said to himself, 'I don't fear God or care about people, but this woman is driving me crazy. I'm going to see that she gets justice, because she is wearing me out with her constant requests!'" Then the Lord said, "Learn a lesson from this unjust judge. Even he rendered a just decision in the end. So don't you think God will surely give justice to his chosen people who cry out to him day and night? Will he keep putting them off? I tell you, he will grant justice to them quickly!"

LUKE 18:1–8 NLT

This parable from Jesus reminds us to never give up hope in our prayers. He urges us to be persistent in prayer. We can cry out to him constantly, day and night, and trust that He will answer.

Dear Jesus, thank You for this story assuring me You never want me to give up hope when I'm praying to You! I will keep on asking for Your help in all things. Amen.

WHAT YOU BELIEVE

Before the mountains were brought forth,
or ever thou hadst formed the earth and the world,
even from everlasting to everlasting, thou art God.
PSALM 90:2 KJV

People once believed the world was flat. This meant only the most intrepid explorers would venture long distances and risk falling off the "edge" of the earth. What people believe determines the choices they make, no matter what era they live in. What do you believe about God? Does it line up with what the Bible says? It's worth checking out. Since you will live what you believe, it's important to be certain what you believe is true.

Jesus, please speak truth and life into my soul.
I want to follow and believe in the one true God.
Show me any lies I may be believing about You.

COMMIT YOUR WAY TO HIM

*Commit your way to the LORD; trust in him and he will do
this: He will make your righteous reward shine like the dawn,
your vindication like the noonday sun. Be still before the LORD
and wait patiently for him; do not fret when people succeed
in their ways, when they carry out their wicked schemes.
Refrain from anger and turn from wrath; do not fret—it
leads only to evil. For those who are evil will be destroyed,
but those who hope in the LORD will inherit the land.*

PSALM 37:5–9 NIV

In a difficult or unfair situation at work or in a relationship,
you may feel hopeless. But take heart and wait patiently for
God to act on your behalf. He sees and knows all the details.
Commit your way to Him with obedience to Him and His Word.
Constantly pray for wisdom and direction. Keep your faith,
stay patient, and maintain your integrity as you trust in Him.
And in His perfect timing He will vindicate and reward you.

*Lord, I'm struggling in this situation, but I know You will
work on my behalf. I commit my way to You as I wait for
Your perfect timing and Your perfect justice. Amen.*

WHOLLY AND COMPLETELY

"Forgive others, and you will be forgiven."
LUKE 6:37 NLT

The words *forgive* and *pardon* come from very old words that mean "to give up completely and wholeheartedly." When we forgive others, we totally give up our rights to feel we've been injured or slighted. And in return, God's grace totally fills the gaps left behind when we let go of our own selfishness. As we give ourselves wholeheartedly to others, God gives Himself completely to us.

God, help me to forgive others so that nothing hinders
me from fully receiving the gift of Your forgiveness.
Thank You for Your grace that pours over me. Amen.

Day 73

THE HOPE TO WHICH HE HAS CALLED YOU

I keep asking that the God of our Lord Jesus Christ, the glorious Father, may give you the Spirit of wisdom and revelation, so that you may know him better. I pray that the eyes of your heart may be enlightened in order that you may know the hope to which he has called you, the riches of his glorious inheritance in his holy people, and his incomparably great power for us who believe. That power is the same as the mighty strength he exerted when he raised Christ from the dead and seated him at his right hand in the heavenly realms.

EPHESIANS 1:17–20 NIV

This prayer of the apostle Paul for the Christians who lived in Ephesus is what God wants for you as a Christian today too. If you believe in Jesus as your only Savior, you belong to Him and you have hope for the awesome things God has planned for you. What's more, His power—the same power that brought Jesus back to life!—is working in you now to help you do the good things God wants for you. That awesome power will be working in you forever, because it has given you eternal life!

Heavenly Father, please help me every day to see and know how awesome You are and how awesome Your plans and Your power in my life are. Increase my faith and hope more and more. Amen.

Day 74

ETERNAL JOY

You make known to me the path of life; you will fill me with joy in your presence, with eternal pleasures at your right hand.
Psalm 16:11 niv

God does not want you to be unhappy and confused. Believe in His grace. He is waiting to show you the way to go. He is longing to give you the joy of His presence. He wants to make you happy forever.

God, You have made Your ways known to me.
All I need to do is trust You and follow You,
and You will lead me to eternal pleasures. Amen.

Day 75

DON'T LET YOUR HANDS
LOSE STRENGTH

*The King of Israel, the Lord, is with you. You will not be
afraid of trouble any more. On that day it will be said
to Jerusalem: "Do not be afraid, O Zion. Do not let your
hands lose their strength. The Lord your God is with
you, a Powerful One Who wins the battle. He will have
much joy over you. With His love He will give you new
life. He will have joy over you with loud singing."*
ZEPHANIAH 3:15–17 NLV

These words through the prophet Zephaniah to the people of
Israel are written down in God's Word to help give you hope
and healing today too. Keep a strong grip on God's hand that
is gripping yours. If you feel yourself start to weaken, focus on
the truth of how great God is in you and hold on tight. Nothing
compares to Him! No one can defeat Him! He will win this
battle you are going through, just *do not let go* of your faith in
Him. All your power and purpose are in Him. Soon, you will be
rejoicing together on the winning side of this hardship and pain.

*Heavenly Father, thank You for Your strong grip
on my life because I believe in You and have been
saved by Your Son. You are my power and purpose.
Help me always hold tightly to You! Amen.*

Day 76

HEALTHY

"Give us today our daily bread."
MATTHEW 6:11 NIV

We need food each day: healthy fruits and vegetables, whole grains, lean protein for our bodies. And we need times of prayer and quiet for our souls. Like a loving mother, God delights in nourishing His children.

Father, You provide everything I need. Help me to make wise choices—to fill myself with healthy foods and the nourishment of Your presence. Amen.

Day 77

INNATE GOODNESS

*I had fainted, unless I had believed to see the
goodness of the LORD in the land of the living.*
PSALM 27:13 KJV

Knowing a friend's heart toward you can help you relax and
be yourself. With a friend like this, you can honestly share
your deepest secrets, feelings, and failures without fear of
ridicule or reprisal. The psalms remind us over and over again
that God's heart toward us is good. Believing in God's innate
goodness means we can entrust every detail of our lives to
Him without hesitation.

*Your Word tells me that I am made holy and righteous
because of Christ in me! I am Your beloved daughter,
and You also call me friend. Thank You for Your great love!*

Day 78

ONE TRUE RELIGION

We need such a Religious Leader Who made the way for man to go to God. Jesus is holy and has no guilt. . . . Christ is not like other religious leaders. They had to give gifts every day on the altar in worship for their own sins first and then for the sins of the people. Christ did not have to do that. He gave one gift on the altar and that gift was Himself. It was done once and it was for all time.

HEBREWS 7:26–27 NLV

Plenty of people might say that all religions are the same, but it's just not true. Our only real hope is belief in Jesus as God and Savior. Jesus alone was perfect and holy and without sin. He is the one and only way, truth, and life (John 14:6). He died as a sacrifice for sin, once, for all people of all time, and He rose to life again—with eyewitness proof. No other religion offers that kind of gift and love and miracle! To know Jesus as Savior is simply to believe in Him and accept His awesome gift of grace and eternal life. He gave this gift when He died on the cross, taking our sins away, and then rose to life again.

Dear Jesus, no one else is like You! You are God and You are Savior, and all my hope is in You! I am so grateful for You! Amen.

SHARING HOPE WITH FUTURE GENERATIONS

*I remember your genuine faith, for you share the faith that
first filled your grandmother Lois and your mother, Eunice.
And I know that same faith continues strong in you.*

2 TIMOTHY 1:5 NLT

The Bible doesn't say much about two women named Lois and
Eunice, but what it does say can inspire us to greater hope for
future generations and motivate us to set wonderful examples
of faith for them. These two women were the grandmother
and mother to a young Christian named Timothy. His friend
was Paul, who wrote many of the letters in the New Testament
of the Bible. The book of 2 Timothy is one of Paul's letters to
Timothy to encourage him in his faith. Paul reminds Timothy
of the true faith of his grandma and his mom, Lois and Eunice.
What an honor for these ladies to be remembered this way!
Think about how you would like your faith to be remembered.
Be strong and keep growing in it so that others will say your
faith was always genuine and will be inspired likewise.

*Heavenly Father, I want to be known for having
true faith in You that I share with future
generations, just like Lois and Eunice. Amen.*

BRAND-NEW WAYS

Intelligent people are always ready to learn.
Their ears are open for knowledge.
PROVERBS 18:15 NLT

Whether you did well in school or not, you probably rely on your intelligence to get you through life. If you're really intelligent, though, you will remember that no matter how many years it has been since you graduated, you are never done learning. You need to be open to new ideas and willing to give up old, stale ways of thinking. When you are, you will find God's grace revealed in brand-new ways.

Father, thank You for the gift of knowledge.
Instill within me a heart that yearns to know more—
more of Your love and more of Your grace. Amen.

WE ARE FROM GOD

We know that everyone who has been born of God does not keep on sinning, but he who was born of God protects him, and the evil one does not touch him. We know that we are from God, and the whole world lies in the power of the evil one. And we know that the Son of God has come and has given us understanding, so that we may know him who is true; and we are in him who is true, in his Son Jesus Christ. He is the true God and eternal life.

1 JOHN 5:18–20 ESV

The evil and sin in this world can feel overwhelming at times. Just trying to follow the news can cause fear and anxiety and depression. But God's Word gives us hope and peace and courage. Yes, the whole world is under the power of the evil one for now—but not forever. And while we wait for Jesus' return to make all things right and new, He protects us and promises us eternal life. We must never forget that we are from God, and greater is He who is in us than he who is in the world (1 John 4:4).

Heavenly Father, please help me not to become overwhelmed and discouraged by the evil and sin in the world. You are always greater than the evil one in the world. Amen.

Day 82

UNFAILING LOVE

But I trust in your unfailing love.
I will rejoice because you have rescued me.
PSALM 13:5 NLT

Have you ever done that exercise in trust where you fall backward into another person's arms? It's hard to let yourself drop, trusting that the other person will catch you. The decision to let yourself fall is not an emotion that sweeps over you. It's just something you have to do despite your fear. In the same way, we commit ourselves to God's unfailing love, finding new joy each time His arms keep us from falling.

Father, You have shown me time and time again that I can trust You because You have consistently rescued me with Your unfailing love. I commit myself to Your loving arms. Amen.

THEY WHO WAIT UPON THE LORD

Have you not known? Have you not heard? The God Who lives forever is the Lord, the One Who made the ends of the earth. He will not become weak or tired. His understanding is too great for us to begin to know. He gives strength to the weak. And He gives power to him who has little strength. Even very young men get tired and become weak and strong young men trip and fall. But they who wait upon the Lord will get new strength. They will rise up with wings like eagles. They will run and not get tired. They will walk and not become weak.

Isaiah 40:28–31 NLV

Imagine never feeling weak or tired! What would you do with all that extra energy and time? With so many activities and stressors in life, our minds just can't fully comprehend it. But our Creator God has endless strength and power. He never falters, and He never fails to share His strength and power with us exactly when we need it. He renews, refreshes, and rejuvenates us time and again—not always according to our preferred schedule but always according to His perfect timeline.

Heavenly Father, fill me with new strength and power when I'm weak and tired. I trust that You can and You will in Your perfect timing. I wait with great hope in You! Amen.

Day 84

EXPRESSIONS OF GRACE

*So I decided there is nothing better than to enjoy food and
drink and to find satisfaction in work. Then I realized
that these pleasures are from the hand of God.*

ECCLESIASTES 2:24 NLT

Hedonists are people who have decided that life's only meaning
lies in physical pleasures. But they can't escape God's hand.
Our food, our drink, the satisfaction we take in our work, and
all the physical pleasures of our lives are not separate from
God. Instead, they are expressions of His grace. He longs for
us to be fulfilled in every way possible.

*Father, all good gifts come from You. You have bestowed
on me pleasures from Your hand. Help me to enjoy them,
and use them to draw me closer to You. Amen.*

YOUR FAVORITE MEAL

But his delight is in the law of the LORD;
and in his law doth he meditate day and night.
PSALM 1:2 KJV

Imagine God's words as your favorite meal, each bite a delicacy to be savored and enjoyed. You relish the unique blend of ingredients, the flavor and texture. When the meal is complete, you're nourished and satisfied. Scripture is a well-balanced meal for your heart and soul, a meal that can continue long after your Bible is back on the shelf. Ponder what you've read. Meditate on God's promises. Chew on the timeless truths that add zest to your life.

Jesus, You are my bread of life. You fill me to overflowing in so many ways. Thank You for providing for my every need!

EVEN WITH UNANSWERED QUESTIONS

That evening they brought to him many who were oppressed by demons, and he cast out the spirits with a word and healed all who were sick. This was to fulfill what was spoken by the prophet Isaiah: "He took our illnesses and bore our diseases."
MATTHEW 8:16–17 ESV

At times, reading the accounts of Jesus' healings might feel discouraging. You believe in the healing power of God and might wonder why He hasn't answered your prayers for healing for yourself or a loved one. Keep crying out to God with those questions. Let your pain and sorrow draw You closer to Him and never drive you away. Ask Him for supernatural comfort and peace and strength in spite of your questions and struggles. His healing is not always what we hope for and expect, but the promise is true that He "heals the brokenhearted and binds up their wounds" (Psalm 147:3 ESV).

Heavenly Father, even when I don't get answers to all of my questions, I choose to keep trusting in You. Pull me back close to You if I ever start to turn away. Even in my pain and sorrow and confusion, I believe You are good and loving and sovereign. In You alone there is victory over sickness and death, and You will make all things new one day soon. Amen.

Day 87

HOPE IN THE ALPHA AND OMEGA

"I am the First and the Last. I am the beginning and the end."
REVELATION 22:13 NLV

Jesus says several times in the Bible that He is the first and the last, the beginning and the end. Some Bible translations use the words *Alpha* and *Omega*; those are the names of the first and last letters in the Greek alphabet. He is *A* and *Z* in our alphabet. Jesus is everything and has always existed. He has gone before us, and He goes ahead of us. He surrounds us on all sides. We struggle to wrap our minds around this truth, but we can rest in the fact that Jesus knows and always has known the whole story of our lives.

*Dear Jesus, You are the beginning and the end of all things.
I am so blessed to call You my hope and my Savior. Amen.*

ASK FOR GOOD GLIMPSES

"No eye has seen, no ear has heard, and no mind has imagined what God has prepared for those who love him." But it was to us that God revealed these things by his Spirit. For his Spirit searches out everything and shows us God's deep secrets.

1 CORINTHIANS 2:9–10 NLT

———

What do you dream and hope for the future? And what do you imagine about heaven? As you dream and imagine, remember 1 Corinthians 2:9–10. We can never fully imagine all the good and awesome things God has planned for us because our human brains just aren't capable! But if we stay strong in our faith in God, we can ask the Holy Spirit within us to show us good glimpses! What good glimpses are you seeing from God these days?

Heavenly Father, I trust that You have amazing plans and blessings for me both here on earth and forever in heaven. Show me glimpses, please! Amen.

YOU BELONG TO THE LORD!

*Be full of joy always because you belong to the Lord.
Again I say, be full of joy! Let all people see how
gentle you are. The Lord is coming again soon.*
PHILIPPIANS 4:4–5 NLV

Be full of joy always? *Ha! Not possible*, you might be thinking.
What's joyful about a broken relationship or a loved one dying?
What's joyful about the loss of a job or a home? What's joyful
about experiencing abuse or neglect, addiction or illness? While
it's true that those things certainly are not joyful, you can still
be full of supernatural joy in the midst of them because of one
important truth: if you trust Jesus as your Savior—you belong
to the Lord! All of those unjoyful things that happen here on
earth are just temporary, but the perfect home God is creating
for us in heaven lasts forever. Jesus is coming again soon, and we
will live there forever with Him—with no suffering ever again!

*Dear Lord, remind me every moment that I belong to
You! That's where my supernatural true joy comes from,
even in the midst of any kind of hardship. Amen.*

CHRISTLIKE

Don't sin by letting anger control you.
Think about it overnight and remain silent.
PSALM 4:4 NLT

A disciple must practice certain skills until she becomes good at them. As Christ's disciples, we are called to live like Him. The challenge of that calling is often hardest in life's small, daily frustrations, especially with the people we love the most. But as we practice saying no to anger, controlling it rather than allowing it to control us, God's grace helps us develop new skills, even ones we never thought possible!

God, teach me the difference between sinful anger
and righteous anger. Help me to push the PAUSE button
when I get angry so that I can listen to You. Amen.

ALWAYS

We accept it always, and in all places. . .with all thankfulness.
ACTS 24:3 KJV

Sometimes we think of gratitude as a polite sort of feeling. After all, as children, we no doubt were taught to say "thank you." But the Bible says that thankfulness is more than being polite. Rather, it is an essential aspect of our lives. We need to learn to consciously cultivate it so that it becomes the framework of our daily lives. Each thing—each person, each event, each place, even each animal—that enters our lives is a gift from a God who loves us so deeply and intimately that we will never be able to grasp the extent of His love, at least not in this life. And so we greet each aspect of our lives not only with acceptance but with thankfulness.

Lord of love, thank You for Your many gifts. Help me to see Your love even in the things that seem hard. Help me to cultivate a constant attitude of gratitude.

HOPE IN THE MIDST OF DANGER

Esther sent this reply to Mordecai: "Go and gather together all the Jews of Susa and fast for me. Do not eat or drink for three days, night or day. My maids and I will do the same. And then, though it is against the law, I will go in to see the king. If I must die, I must die."
ESTHER 4:15–16 NLT

Esther could have been killed for her boldness in speaking up to the king in defense of her people. But she hoped and trusted in the one true God. And because of her courage, her people, the Jews, were saved from the destruction intended by Haman's evil plans. Take time soon to read the whole book of Esther, and then anytime you need some extra faith and hope and courage, ask God to remind you of Esther's story and how He worked out His good plans to protect His people through her.

Heavenly Father, I want to have the courage of Esther in any hard or dangerous situation I face. Fill me up with trust in Your power and perfect plans. Amen.

ALL THE DAYS OF YOUR LIFE

*O Lord, you alone are my hope. I've trusted you,
O Lord, from childhood. Yes, you have been with me
from birth; from my mother's womb you have cared
for me. No wonder I am always praising you!*
Psalm 71:5–6 nlt

Think of all the people throughout your life, from the time you were born until now, whom God has provided to care for you and bond with you. Praise Him for all those people and for His love! Ultimately, God is the one who constantly watches over you, and He works through many different people to care for you. He always has and always will. Believe this promise from Psalm 23:6 (esv): "Surely goodness and mercy shall follow me all the days of my life, and I shall dwell in the house of the Lord forever."

Dear Lord, thank You for the people You have placed in my life, some for just a season and some for the long haul, who care for me and connect with me with love that ultimately comes from You! I trust that Your goodness and mercy will follow me daily and that You will always provide me with the people I need in my life. Amen.

Day 94

PEACE

"I will teach all your children, and they will enjoy great peace."
ISAIAH 54:13 NLT

It's hard not to worry about the children in our lives. Many dangers threaten them, and our world is so uncertain. We can do our best to teach and guide the children we love, but in the end we must trust them to God's grace, knowing that they must find their own relationship with Him—and that as they know Him, they will find peace, even in the midst of the world's uncertainty.

Heavenly Father, thank You for the children in my life.
Help me to remember that You love them even more than
I do and that You hold them in Your loving arms. Amen.

Day 95

RICHNESS

*Let the message about Christ, in all its richness,
fill your lives. . . . Sing psalms and hymns and
spiritual songs to God with thankful hearts.*
Colossians 3:16 NLT

The more we think about Christ and all He has done for us,
the more gratitude will fill our lives. Because of His love for us,
we not only have eternal life but have a life filled to the brim
with blessings right now. Because of Christ, we are free from
the guilt and anxiety of sin. Because of Christ, we can come
close to God; we even have God living within our hearts, knit
into the fabric of our being. The more we ponder this reality,
the more the richness of our lives in Christ just naturally spills
over into a song of thankfulness.

*I am so grateful, Christ, for the immense richness of all You have
done for me. May my life be filled with songs of praise to You.*

STORY OF GOD'S LOVE

Thy testimonies are wonderful:
therefore doth my soul keep them.
PSALM 119:129 KJV

The Bible isn't a novel to be read for entertainment, a textbook to be skimmed for knowledge, a manual for living, or a collection of inspirational sayings. The Bible is a love letter. It's the story of God's love for His children from the beginning of the world until the end—and beyond. It's a book that takes time to know well, but God promises His own Spirit will help us understand what we read. All we need to do is ask.

Holy Spirit, I ask You to fill me with love,
wisdom, and understanding as You teach
and convict me from Your Word.

IN ALL OUR TROUBLES

Praise be to the God and Father of our Lord Jesus Christ, the Father of compassion and the God of all comfort, who comforts us in all our troubles, so that we can comfort those in any trouble with the comfort we ourselves receive from God. For just as we share abundantly in the sufferings of Christ, so also our comfort abounds through Christ.

2 Corinthians 1:3–5 niv

God's Word promises that we will be comforted in all our troubles. And that there is purpose in all our troubles, even when they seem so senseless. Whatever hardship or pain we go through, we receive abundant comfort from God that fills us up to overflowing so that we can pour it out onto others who need comfort. We must never turn away from God in times of trouble. Rather, we must draw all the closer to Him, share in the sufferings of Christ, and lay hold of the camaraderie and compassion we find there so that we are full and ready to care well for others as God leads us.

Heavenly Father, I praise You for the compassion and comfort You show me in every trial and heartache. Fill me up to overflowing and help me share Your comfort with others so they too can know Your great love and salvation. Amen.

HOPE IN SUFFERING

In his kindness God called you to share in his eternal glory by means of Christ Jesus. So after you have suffered a little while, he will restore, support, and strengthen you, and he will place you on a firm foundation. All power to him forever! Amen.

1 PETER 5:10–11 NLT

Suffering in our earthly life is inevitable but not endless. As this scripture promises, after you've experienced suffering, God will restore you, support you, strengthen you, and place you on a firm foundation once again. Let this promise give you hope in the midst of your trial and pain today. It will not last forever. Keep moving forward; keep holding tightly to faith in our Savior. In His perfect timing, He will rescue you from it, and during it, He will never leave you.

Heavenly Father, I know You have all power to rescue me from this suffering in my life, and I trust You will at exactly the right time. Show me Your presence and encouragement in the midst of it. Amen.

Day 99

BLESSING OTHERS

"Bless those who curse you. Pray for those who hurt you."
LUKE 6:28 NLT

Not only does God bless us but we are called to bless others. God wants to show the world His grace through us. He can do this when we show our commitment to make God's love real in the world around us through our words and actions, as well as through our prayer life. We offer blessings to others when we greet a scowl with a smile, when we refuse to respond to angry words, and when we offer understanding to those who are angry and hurt.

God, I sometimes forget that the world is watching. I long to shine Your light to everyone I see. Help me to bestow blessings on others, even when they hurt me. Amen.

ROOTS

Let your roots grow down into him, and let your lives be built on him. Then your faith will grow strong in the truth you were taught, and you will overflow with thankfulness.
COLOSSIANS 2:7 NLT

Life is uncertain. Our world is full of so many dangers, so much unrest, so many arguments, and so much fear and anger. In the midst of all that, it can be hard to keep our balance. It's easy to feel as though we're at sea in the middle of a storm, being tossed back and forth. But the Bible tells us we don't have to live like that. Instead, we can grow deep roots anchored firmly in God. When our lives are built on Him, we will no longer lose our balance because of the world's dangers and unrest. Our faith will grow strong—and our hearts will overflow with thankfulness.

God, I am so grateful that You are helping me to grow deep roots in You. I know that no matter what is happening in the world, I don't need to be afraid.

Day 101

GOD'S BLESSINGS

Return unto thy rest, O my soul;
*for the L*ORD *hath dealt bountifully with thee.*
PSALM 116:7 KJV

"Friends know what friends need," so the saying goes. That's one reason why friends often throw baby showers for moms-to-be. It's a way to help provide what a mom will need in the months to come. God knows us, and our needs, better than any friend or family member. That's why He throws us a shower every day. God wraps His blessings in wisdom, purpose, and creativity to help meet our physical, emotional, and spiritual needs.

Father, help me to rest in the truth of who You are.
You are my provider. Help me stop striving to meet my
own needs and, instead, let You be Lord of my life.

HOPE FOR A HOPELESS WIDOW

Then the word of the LORD came to [Elijah]: "Go at once
to Zarephath in the region of Sidon and stay there.
I have directed a widow there to supply you with food."
1 KINGS 17:8–9 NIV

When the prophet Elijah found the widow, she told him she didn't have any bread—just a little bit of flour and oil. She was certain that she was about to make the very last tiny meal for her son and herself and that they would soon starve to death. Maybe you also have experienced that kind of desperate resignation, either physically or spiritually, or both. But with God, you always have hope. He can provide and rescue, just as He did through Elijah for the widow of Zarephath. She obeyed the instruction from God through His prophet and chose to trust that He would continue to provide for her and her son after she provided for Elijah first. Later on, she was rewarded far more greatly when, after her son tragically died, Elijah brought him back to life through God's miracle-working power.

Heavenly Father, when I feel desperate with no hope, remind me of Elijah and the widow. I pray that You will provide and heal and rescue in miraculous ways. I believe You can and will! Amen.

Day 103

REMEMBER GOD'S RED SEA MIRACLE

*Moses stretched out his hand over the sea, and the LORD drove
the sea back by a strong east wind all night and made the
sea dry land, and the waters were divided. And the people of
Israel went into the midst of the sea on dry ground, the waters
being a wall to them on their right hand and on their left.*

EXODUS 14:21–22 ESV

What an awesome miracle—God's parting of the Red Sea to
rescue His people from the Egyptians pursuing them. What an
astounding sight that must have been! Walls of water on the
left and right and dry ground to walk on in the midst of the
sea? Just unreal! And the same God who parted the waters
is the one who sees and knows and loves you right now. He
is awesome beyond your wildest imagination, and He is able
to make a way through whatever Red Sea kind of problem or
pain you need to cross right now. Praise Him for His greatness
and goodness and power. Keep hoping and trusting in Him!

*Heavenly Father, You are amazing beyond description.
I trust that You can do absolutely anything to rescue Your
people, including me! All my hope is in You! Amen.*

Day 104

A FUTURE AND A HOPE

*"'For I know the plans I have for you,' says the Lord,
'plans for well-being and not for trouble, to give you a
future and a hope. Then you will call upon Me and come
and pray to Me, and I will listen to you. You will look for Me
and find Me, when you look for Me with all your heart.'"*
JEREMIAH 29:11–13 NLV

Let these words spoken through the prophet Jeremiah to the people of Israel encourage you as you ask God to show you His specific plans for your future. Look back and thank Him for how He has guided you in the past to provide for you and bless you. Acknowledge and repent of those times when you went your own way instead of following His lead. And remember that, no matter what twists and turns life takes here on earth, the best future and hope that God is planning for you is forever in heaven.

*Dear Lord, I call upon You! Please lead me in the good
plans You have for me. Help me not to go my own way.
Help me to look for You with all my heart. Amen.*

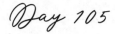

TRUTHS

It exposes our innermost thoughts and desires.
HEBREWS 4:12 NLT

God's words are not merely letters on a page. They are living things that work their way into our hearts and minds, revealing the fears and hopes we've kept hidden away—sometimes even from ourselves. Like a doctor's scalpel that cuts in order to heal, God's Word slices through our carefully created facades and exposes our deepest truths.

Father, how grateful I am for Your Word. I am amazed at the way it teaches me and exposes my true intentions. Help me to bravely submit myself to Your healing. Amen.

FOOD

God created those foods to be eaten with thanks
by faithful people who know the truth.
1 TIMOTHY 4:3 NLT

We live in a world where both dieting and overeating are like the two sides of a double-edged sword. Our society tells us that we need to be thin; we need to look a certain way in order to measure up (and most of us have bumps and bulges that we wish would go away). At the same time, food—and a lot of it—plays a very important role in our social activities. Often, we turn to food when we are bored or sad or nervous, and then we feel guilty and anxious because we believe we should be eating less. The Bible, however, points us in a different direction when it comes to food. Food is a gift from God, and we are to give thanks for it. It's that simple.

Lord, heal my attitudes toward food. May I remember that each thing I eat is a gift from You. Take away both my overindulgence and my guilt, and replace them with thankfulness.

LET THE TEARS FALL

You keep track of all my sorrows. You have collected all my tears in your bottle. You have recorded each one in your book.
PSALM 56:8 NLT

Not even our most devoted loved ones can possibly care for us as much as our heavenly Father does. Only He can literally keep track of every single tear we cry. Whatever pain and problems you are going through, take time to let yourself release the emotions. Don't hold them in, and don't think they don't matter to anyone. Let the tears fall freely—and instead of bottling them up inside yourself, let God be the one to bottle them up and comfort you in the midst of the sorrow. Trust His Word that "those who plant in tears will harvest with shouts of joy" (Psalm 126:5 NLT).

Heavenly Father, remind me as I let the tears fall that they never fall in vain. You keep track of my tears because You care about me that much, and You are healing me and giving me hope even in the midst of them. Amen.

YOU CAN ALWAYS BE SURE OF GOD

The Lord is my light and the One Who saves me. Whom should I fear? The Lord is the strength of my life. Of whom should I be afraid? When sinful men, and all who hated me, came against me to destroy my flesh, they tripped and fell. Even if an army gathers against me, my heart will not be afraid. Even if war rises against me, I will be sure of You.

PSALM 27:1–3 NLV

Let this psalm give you strength and confidence and hope! With the Lord as your light and as the one who saves you, nothing and no one should ever make you feel afraid. There's not a lot in this world you can be sure of these days, but you can always be absolutely sure of Him—sure of His power and protection and provision for you and especially sure of His great love for you!

Heavenly Father, thank You that I can be totally, completely, 100 percent sure of You! Amen.

Day 109

FOCUS POINT

Therefore. . .stand firm. Let nothing move you.
1 CORINTHIANS 15:58 NIV

Some days, stress comes at us from all directions. Our emotions are overwhelming. Life makes us dizzy. On days like that, don't worry about getting a lot accomplished—and don't try to make enormous leaps in your spiritual life. Instead, simply stand in one place. Like a ballet dancer who looks at one point to keep her balance while she twirls, fix your eyes on Jesus.

Jesus, when I get caught up in the whirlwind of stress and busyness and my own agenda, I can easily lose my balance. Help me to fix my eyes on You. Amen.

WORDS AS BLESSINGS

*God be merciful unto us, and bless us;
and cause his face to shine upon us.*
PSALM 67:1 KJV

When people speak of "blessings," they're often referring to words. Blessings are given at meals and weddings. "Bless you" is even said after a sneeze. The words we say can be as much of a gift as the blessings we can hold in our hands. What would God have you say to the people you meet today? Consider how you can bless others with your words—then speak up. A good word can often be the perfect gift.

*Lord, allow me to bless others with my life,
my actions, and my words. I want to bring life and
blessing to people. Show me what that looks like.*

FAMILY MATTERS

*Those who won't care for their relatives, especially
those in their own household, have denied the true
faith. Such people are worse than unbelievers.*
1 TIMOTHY 5:8 NLT

Family matters to God. He has placed you in the family you have, and He expects you and your loved ones to take care of each other. He also knows that family relationships can be strained and broken and in desperate need of healing. If all parties involved humbly ask for and use God's help and wisdom, they can do their best to work things out with forgiveness and grace and love for each other. All families need to apply this scripture liberally: "Put on then, as God's chosen ones, holy and beloved, compassionate hearts, kindness, humility, meekness, and patience, bearing with one another and, if one has a complaint against another, forgiving each other; as the Lord has forgiven you, so you also must forgive. And above all these put on love, which binds everything together in perfect harmony" (Colossians 3:12–14 ESV).

*Heavenly Father, thank You for my family.
Please help us to love each other and take care of
each other the way You want us to. Amen.*

LITTLE GIRL, GET UP!

When they came to the home of the synagogue leader, Jesus saw much commotion and weeping and wailing. He went inside and asked, "Why all this commotion and weeping? The child isn't dead; she's only asleep." The crowd laughed at him. But he made them all leave, and he took the girl's father and mother and his three disciples into the room where the girl was lying. Holding her hand, he said to her, "Talitha koum," which means "Little girl, get up!" And the girl, who was twelve years old, immediately stood up and walked around! They were overwhelmed and totally amazed.

MARK 5:38–42 NLT

We don't know what illness Jairus' daughter had that made her so sick that she died, but we can tell that she was dearly loved by her dad and mom and many others. Her dad had great faith that Jesus could come and simply put His hand on her and she would live. And he was right. Jesus went home with Jairus to the room were his daughter lay. He took her by the hand and with just one short command—"Little girl, get up!"—she was healthy and whole!

Heavenly Father, You are the amazing God of life and miracles! Thank You for the awesome ways Jesus has showed us Your love and power to heal and give life. Amen.

TRUST

The LORD is my strength and shield. I trust him with all my heart. He helps me, and my heart is filled with joy. I burst out in songs of thanksgiving.
PSALM 28:7 NLT

Gratitude and trust are intimately linked together. The more we trust God, the more thankful we will feel for His love and care. The more we practice thankfulness for all God has done and is doing in our lives, the more we will trust Him. The two things just naturally go together. God helps us with our daily lives—and our hearts spontaneously spill over with joy and gratitude. Living in this state of continual glad thankfulness takes practice, though. We can choose to dwell on all that is "wrong" with our lives—or we can choose to see life from the perspective of trust and gratitude.

*Teach me, I pray, to trust You more, Lord.
Help me to see all that You are doing in my life.
May my heart burst out in songs of gratitude.*

CASTING BURDENS

Cast thy burden upon the LORD, and he shall sustain thee.
PSALM 55:22 KJV

Casting a fishing line is an almost effortless motion. Casting a burden paints a totally different image. Burdens are pictured as heavy, cumbersome, not easily carried—let alone "cast." But casting our burdens on God is as easy as speaking to Him in prayer. It's calling for help when we need it, admitting our sin when we've fallen, and letting our tears speak for our hearts when words fail us.

When my heart is heavy, Lord, You are the only one who can help. I lay these burdens at Your feet, trusting that You will carry them for me as I rest in You.

THROUGH EVERYTHING GOD HAS MADE

*Ever since the world was created, people have seen the earth
and sky. Through everything God made, they can clearly
see his invisible qualities—his eternal power and divine
nature. So they have no excuse for not knowing God.*

ROMANS 1:20 NLT

At times, we might feel hopeless and wonder if we are doing
enough to help people learn about God and have a chance to
be saved. But God promises in His Word that He has shown
Himself through everything He has made in creation. Therefore,
no one can say they know nothing about God. Everyone can
see Him in the tiny details of a pretty flower and in the highest
peaks of a rocky mountain range. He can be seen in everything
from the incredible design of our human bodies to the ingenu-
ity that animals show in building homes for themselves. Our
Creator God is awesome and worthy of all our praise!

*Heavenly Father, thank You for making Yourself known. I pray
that more people will want to grow closer to You through
Jesus as a result of seeing Your goodness in creation. Amen.*

Day 116

YOUR SAFE PLACE

*My soul is quiet and waits for God alone. My hope comes
from Him. He alone is my rock and the One Who saves me.
He is my strong place. I will not be shaken. My being safe
and my honor rest with God. My safe place is in God, the
rock of my strength. Trust in Him at all times, O people.
Pour out your heart before Him. God is a safe place for us.*
PSALM 62:5–8 NLV

When you think of your safe place, do you think of the place
you feel most comfortable and relaxed and understood? Maybe
you think of being at home with your family, cozy and secure.
Or maybe you think of being with your best friend—the person
you can talk to about anything. Those are wonderful safe
places, but God wants to be your very best, strongest, most
secure safe place! He is with you anytime and anywhere. Talk
to Him, cry out to Him, depend on Him, and trust Him for
everything you need.

*Heavenly Father, You are my solid rock and safe place
everywhere I go and in every situation I encounter. Thank You
that I can pour out my heart to You anytime, anywhere. Amen.*

HEAVEN'S PERSPECTIVE

Always give yourselves fully to the work of the Lord,
because you know that your labor in the Lord is not in vain.
1 CORINTHIANS 15:58 NIV

You may feel sometimes as though all of your hard work comes to nothing. But if your work is the Lord's work, you can trust Him to bring it to fulfillment. You may not always know what is being accomplished in the light of eternity, but God knows. And when you look back from heaven's perspective, you will be able to see how much grace was accomplished through all of your hard work.

God, when I don't see results, I sometimes get
discouraged in my work for You. Help me to remember
that You are busy doing things I cannot see. Amen.

WORRY

Don't worry about anything; instead, pray about everything.
Tell God what you need, and thank him for all he has done.
PHILIPPIANS 4:6 NLT

Did you know that the very earliest Old English meaning of *worry* was "to strangle"? It literally meant "to seize by the throat and tear." That's how destructive worry can be. It can rip away our sense of peace and well-being. It can make us lose sleep and rob our days of joy. But the Bible says there is an antidote to worry: prayer and gratitude. The more we pray about our concerns, giving them to God and thanking Him for His work in our lives, the less room we will have in our minds for worry. Anxiety and gratitude can't exist in the same place in our heads.

Heavenly Father, when worry begins to consume
my mind, remind me that there's a way out.
Turn my attention to prayer and gratitude.

Day 119

NEVER ALONE

*Blessed be the Lord, who daily loadeth us with
benefits, even the God of our salvation.*
PSALM 68:19 KJV

Some things are too heavy to carry alone. A couch, for instance.
Or a washing machine. The same is true for the mental and
emotional burdens we bear. The good news is that strength,
peace, comfort, hope, and a host of other helping hands are
only a prayer away. We're never alone in our pain or struggle.
God is always near, right beside us, ready to help carry what's
weighing us down.

*Lord, You know the heaviness in my heart. Some days
it feels like more than I can bear. Please take these
feelings and issues. Help me trust that You are bigger.*

TAKE HEART, DAUGHTER

Just then a woman who had been subject to bleeding for twelve years came up behind him and touched the edge of his cloak. She said to herself, "If I only touch his cloak, I will be healed." Jesus turned and saw her. "Take heart, daughter," he said, "your faith has healed you." And the woman was healed at that moment.

MATTHEW 9:20–22 NIV

If you've ever had a sickness that dragged on and on, you know how sick of being sick you get, even for a matter of days or weeks. The poor bleeding woman in the Bible had been sick for twelve *years*! But she had heard of Jesus, and she had great faith in His power. She was sure that if she could just touch the edge of His cloak, she would be healed. So she did, and she was! Jesus is saying the same words to you today—whatever you're going through: "Take heart, daughter. Your faith has healed you." Even if not at this moment or even in this life, Jesus will heal you forever in heaven.

Dear Jesus, I take heart and have hope in You alone. You have all power to heal and to give eternal life. I praise You for this awesome truth! Amen.

DON'T NEGLECT MEETING TOGETHER

*Let us hold tightly without wavering to the hope we affirm,
for God can be trusted to keep his promise. Let us think
of ways to motivate one another to acts of love and good
works. And let us not neglect our meeting together, as
some people do, but encourage one another, especially
now that the day of his return is drawing near.*

HEBREWS 10:23–25 NLT

In a world full of sadness and pain, sin and temptation, and
Satan's lies and schemes, we Christians must intentionally and
firmly keep our grip on our hope in Jesus Christ. We must constantly remind each other of it and encourage each other in it.
That's why being part of a true, whole-Bible-teaching church
is so important. We need regular fellowship and support so we
can encourage each other to never let go of hope and motivate
each other in acts of love and good works that will spread our
faith in Jesus to others so they might trust in Him too.

*Heavenly Father, I trust Your promises and want to
hold tightly to my hope in You through Your Son, Jesus
Christ. Help me to have fellowship with other believers
that encourages and motivates both me and them and
also spreads hope to others around us. Amen.*

GRACE MULTIPLIED

*Honor the LORD with your wealth and with
the best part of everything you produce.*
PROVERBS 3:9 NLT

We connect the word *wealth* with money, but long ago, the word meant "happiness, prosperity, well-being." If you think about your wealth in this light, then the word encompasses far more of your life. Your health, your abilities, your friends, your family, your physical strength, and your creative energy—all of these are parts of your true wealth. Grace brought all of these riches into your life, and when we use them to honor God, grace is multiplied still more.

*Father, when I consider all the good things You
have given me, I am rich beyond belief. Help me to
graciously honor You with my wealth. Amen.*

JOYFUL NOISE

Let us come before his presence with thanksgiving,
and make a joyful noise unto him with psalms.
PSALM 95:2 KJV

Thankfulness is an inner feeling—but to have its full effect in us, it needs to spill over into our outer lives where others can see it. There are all kinds of ways we can make a "joyful noise." It might be a song we hum while we do our work, but it could just as easily be a note of happiness that others can hear in our voices when we speak. Many times it won't be a literal noise. It might be the ease with which we laugh, or even just a smile on our faces. It could be words we write in emails or texts or the lightness of our feet as we go about our work.

I want to live my life in Your presence, dear God,
a place that puts a song on my lips, a smile
on my face, and a dance in my step.

Day 124

RENEWED STRENGTH

Great is our Lord, and of great power: his understanding is infinite. The LORD lifteth up the meek.
PSALM 147:5–6 KJV

During a track-and-field event, it isn't uncommon to see an athlete trip over one of the hurdles and tumble to the ground. What brings the crowd to its feet is when the runner gets back up. Challenge involves risk, in sports and in life. Don't be afraid of trying difficult things. Whether you succeed or fail, God promises to renew your strength and purpose. You may not understand how, but you can be certain He's able.

God, I have failed so much in my life. I pray that You would use all of those failures in a way that brings glory to You and draws others to Your heart.

HIS ANGELS WILL HOLD YOU UP

He will order his angels to protect you wherever
you go. They will hold you up with their hands so
you won't even hurt your foot on a stone.
PSALM 91:11–12 NLT

The stories we hear about people experiencing angels some-times seem like far-fetched fiction, but no matter the way some stories might be embellished, the Bible says angels are real. God helps us and protects us through their watch and care over our lives. Psalm 103:20–21 (NLT) says, "Praise the LORD, you angels, you mighty ones who carry out his plans, listening for each of his commands. Yes, praise the LORD, you armies of angels who serve him and do his will!"

Heavenly Father, thank You for Your mighty angels who obey
Your commands and who watch over me. I feel secure and loved
and hopeful because of Your care and protection. Amen.

GOD'S HAND

Even if I walk into trouble, You will keep my life safe. You will put out Your hand against the anger of those who hate me. And Your right hand will save me. The Lord will finish the work He started for me. O Lord, Your loving-kindness lasts forever.
PSALM 138:7–8 NLV

Is there anyone in your life who truly seems to hate you? Anyone purposefully trying to put you in danger or make your life miserable? Do you feel like the situation will never get better? If that's the case, remember and pray this scripture. God will keep your life safe in any kind of trouble. He can put out His hand to protect you against any danger or malice from anyone who might treat you hatefully. Pray to ask Him to do so, and thank and praise Him when He does!

Heavenly Father, I feel hated by some people right now, and I'm overwhelmed. Please put out Your hand against them to protect and save me. I trust in Your everlasting love and kindness. Amen.

QUIET, GENTLE GRACE

*"Let me teach you, because I am humble and gentle
at heart, and you will find rest for your souls."*
MATTHEW 11:29 NLT

Sometimes we keep trying to do things on our own, even though
we don't know what we're doing or we're exhausted. And all
the while, Jesus waits quietly, ready to show us the way. He
will lead us with quiet, gentle grace, carrying our burdens for
us. We don't have to try so hard. We can finally rest.

*Jesus, I don't like feeling incompetent and inadequate.
It makes me feel anxious and exhausted. Thank
You for Your gentle teaching and for the strength
You provide. Give me Your rest. Amen.*

COMMUNAL THANKSGIVING

All this is for your benefit, so that the grace that is reaching more and more people may cause thanksgiving to overflow to the glory of God.
2 CORINTHIANS 4:15 NIV

God is good to each of us individually, and we each have our own unique relationship with Him. This means that gratitude may be a private, individual feeling we carry in our hearts. At the same time, though, we are called to live in community, and the Holy Spirit spreads grace to us all. In this sense, gratitude is communal. It's something we experience together, and it's something we express together. As we do, we amplify gratitude. We feel it more intensely as individuals—and it spreads from us to others.

Thank You, Lord of love, that Your grace has no limits. May it spill through me to others. Make us, I pray, a community knit together by gratitude.

Day 129

WHEN YOUR HEART IS SAD

Why am I discouraged? Why is my heart so sad? I will put my hope in God! I will praise him again—my Savior and my God!
PSALM 42:11 NLT

When we put our hope in anything other than God, we will always end up discouraged and sad. We might find temporary encouragement and happiness, but it won't last. First John 2:17 (NLT) says, "This world is fading away, along with everything that people crave. But anyone who does what pleases God will live forever." And that forever life that God guarantees is our motivation and a source of real hope and real encouragement. It's the reason we can have true, lasting, deep-down joy, not just fickle, fleeting happiness.

My Savior and my God, I put all my hope in You and I praise You! Remind me that when I'm feeling discouraged and sad, it's because my attention is not on You and the forever life You promise. When my heart is downcast and heavy, please lighten it and lift it back to You. Amen.

REMEMBER ANNA

Anna, a prophet, was also there in the Temple. She was the daughter of Phanuel from the tribe of Asher, and she was very old. Her husband died when they had been married only seven years. Then she lived as a widow to the age of eighty-four. She never left the Temple but stayed there day and night, worshiping God with fasting and prayer. She came along just as Simeon was talking with Mary and Joseph, and she began praising God. She talked about the child to everyone who had been waiting expectantly for God to rescue Jerusalem.

LUKE 2:36–38 NLT

Anna lost her husband after only a short marriage and surely must have suffered with grief. But she found hope and healing through total devotion to God with day-and-night worship through fasting and prayer. What a blessing that she was able to see the infant Jesus, the long-awaited Messiah, with her own eyes!

Heavenly Father, when I suffer loss, remind me through Anna's example that great hope and healing can be found through spending my time devoted to You in worship, fasting, and prayer. Please bless me as You blessed Anna. Amen.

Day 131

WAITING FOR THE LORD

I did not give up waiting for the Lord. And He turned to me and heard my cry. He brought me up out of the hole of danger, out of the mud and clay. He set my feet on a rock, making my feet sure. He put a new song in my mouth, a song of praise to our God. Many will see and fear and will put their trust in the Lord.
PSALM 40:1–3 NLV

It's hard to be patient while we wait with hope. But even when it seems like it's taking God forever to answer your prayers, don't give up. At just the right time, He will answer and help you according to His will. And like this psalm says, He will bring you out of danger and onto solid rock. Then you'll be singing new songs to God—and many will see what happened and hear your praise and put their trust in God too! Remember that your patient, steadfast faith sets an example for others to hope in God as well.

Heavenly Father, I want to have patient, steadfast faith. I never want to give up on waiting for You. Please help me to keep hanging on, waiting with joyful hope for Your perfect timing and plans. Amen.

Day 132

MOVE ON

Anyone who belongs to Christ has become a new person. The old life is gone; a new life has begun!
2 CORINTHIANS 5:17 NLT

You are a brand-new person in Jesus! Don't worry about what came before. Don't linger over your guilt and regret. Move on. Step out into the new, grace-filled life Christ has given you.

Heavenly Father, how grateful I am for new life! Thank You for putting to death the old me and for giving me the promise of a new life in Christ. Amen.

ACHIEVING THE IMPOSSIBLE

The LORD is nigh unto all them that call upon him, to all that call upon him in truth.
PSALM 145:18 KJV

Some mornings you wake up with the knowledge that a challenging day is ahead of you. Other times, difficulty catches you by surprise. Whatever challenge enters your life, remind yourself that the Lord is near. Not only will God help you meet each challenge head-on but He will use each one to help you grow. Look for God's hand at work in your life, helping you achieve what may seem impossible.

My heart is set on You, Lord. Be my eyes and ears this day. Use each challenge for Your purposes. Help me see Your hand in everything.

PROVING YOUR FAITH
AND SHARING HOPE

*There is wonderful joy ahead, even though you must endure
many trials for a little while. These trials will show that your
faith is genuine. It is being tested as fire tests and purifies
gold—though your faith is far more precious than mere gold.
So when your faith remains strong through many trials,
it will bring you much praise and glory and honor on the
day when Jesus Christ is revealed to the whole world.*

1 PETER 1:6–7 NLT

When we keep our faith in Jesus as our Savior through all kinds
of pain and hardship, we prove our faith is real and set an example
of hope for others. Saying we love and trust Jesus during
good times is easy, but saying we love and trust Him even when
we go through bad times is not. Your faith is the most valuable
thing about you, worth so much more than gold or any kind
of treasure. So keep asking God to grow and strengthen it, and
don't be surprised that it will be tested sometimes. Hold on to
God during those testing times and see how your faith develops
an extraordinary new shine that helps light the way for others.

*Heavenly Father, please help me to pass the tests of my faith
well. I want to keep holding on to You—proving that my faith
is genuine and sharing my hope in You with others! Amen.*

HELP FROM THE MAKER OF HEAVEN AND EARTH

I lift up my eyes to the mountains—where does my help come from? My help comes from the LORD, the Maker of heaven and earth. He will not let your foot slip—he who watches over you will not slumber; indeed, he who watches over Israel will neither slumber nor sleep. The LORD watches over you—the LORD is your shade at your right hand; the sun will not harm you by day, nor the moon by night. The LORD will keep you from all harm—he will watch over your life.

PSALM 121:1–7 NIV

When you feel hopeless, look up! Remember where your help comes from—the Maker of heaven and earth! Fix your thoughts on His greatness and His devoted care of you. Worship and praise Him! He never tires or falters in watching over you. You can rest well because He never takes a rest. He will keep you from all harm.

Dear Lord, I look up to You for my help and hope. And at night, I lie down in peace, knowing You never stop watching over me. Thank You! Amen.

JUST ABIDE

"Already you are clean because of the word that I have spoken to you. Abide in me, and I in you. As the branch cannot bear fruit by itself, unless it abides in the vine, neither can you, unless you abide in me. I am the vine; you are the branches. Whoever abides in me and I in him, he it is that bears much fruit, for apart from me you can do nothing."

JOHN 15:3–5 ESV

Jesus described Himself as a vine and God the Father as the gardener. We are the branches. The fruit we grow on our branches consists of the good things we do for God that He has planned for us—like serving and caring for others, sharing God's love, and helping others to know Jesus as Savior. At times in life, we may become discouraged, feeling as if we aren't producing enough good fruit. But Jesus says simply to abide in Him—and, as a result of that relationship, we will produce plenty according to His will. We don't have to worry and wonder about the size of the crop; we simply focus on loving our Savior and staying close to Him, getting life from Him. Then He will make the fruit grow.

Dear Jesus, my life is from You and for You. I want to abide in close relationship with You. Keep me close and grow in me the good fruit You want to produce through my life in You! Amen.

Day 137

THE GATEWAY TO GOD'S PRESENCE

Enter into his gates with thanksgiving, and into his courts with praise: be thankful unto him, and bless his name.

PSALM 100:4 KJV

Sometimes we get the idea that God's presence is a solemn, sober place, a place with few smiles and little laughter. When we give others that impression, following Christ doesn't look like much fun. The Bible tells us, though, that the gate into God's presence is the practice of joyful thanksgiving. Gratitude is the certain entryway into His courts. The more we thank Him, the closer we will draw to Him. The more we praise Him, the more we will be aware of His sure and constant presence in our lives.

Thank You, God, for all You do for me.
Thank You for Your love. Thank You for Your continual
presence. Teach me to always bless Your name.

MULTIPLIED

"There will be joy and songs of thanksgiving, and I will multiply my people, not diminish them; I will honor them, not despise them. . . . You will be my people, and I will be your God."
JEREMIAH 30:19, 22 NLT

Sometimes we talk about following Christ as though it were all about giving up things. We act as though the Christian life consists of "don'ts" and "shall nots." But the Bible assures us that God doesn't want to diminish our lives. Instead, He wants to expand them. He wants to multiply our blessings. When we fully realize that we are God's and that He is ours, then we will begin to see His love everywhere we turn. And the more we express our gratitude to Him, the sharper our spiritual vision will become.

Lord, I want to sing You a song of thanksgiving for all the ways You have blessed and multiplied my life.

TOTAL TRANSFORMATION

Meanwhile, Saul was uttering threats with every breath and was eager to kill the Lord's followers. So he went to the high priest. He requested letters addressed to the synagogues in Damascus, asking for their cooperation in the arrest of any followers of the Way he found there. He wanted to bring them—both men and women—back to Jerusalem in chains. As he was approaching Damascus on this mission, a light from heaven suddenly shone down around him. He fell to the ground and heard a voice saying to him, "Saul! Saul! Why are you persecuting me?" "Who are you, lord?" Saul asked. And the voice replied, "I am Jesus, the one you are persecuting! Now get up and go into the city, and you will be told what you must do."

Acts 9:1–6 nlt

No matter the sin people get themselves involved in, even the persecution and murder of innocent people, hope can be found in Jesus Christ. The story of Saul, later called Paul, is a prime example of this truth. Jesus called him out of his evil life and completely turned his life around. And Jesus is still in the business of doing total transformations today.

Dear Jesus, I have great faith in Your power to totally transform any person and call them out of any kind of sinful lifestyle. I praise You for Your awesome work as the one true Savior! Amen.

SEE JESUS

God left nothing that is not subject to them. Yet at present we do not see everything subject to them. But we do see Jesus.
HEBREWS 2:8–9 NIV

We know that Jesus has won the victory over sin. Yet when we look at the world as it is right now, we still see sin all around us. We see pain and suffering, greed and selfishness, brokenness and despair. We know that the world is not ruled by God. Despite that, we can look past the darkness of sin. By grace, right now, we can see Jesus.

Jesus, when I am overwhelmed by the evil that seems to be winning in this world, remind me that You have won the victory. Give me the grace to see You. Amen.

THANKFUL TALK

Though some tongues just love the taste of gossip,
those who follow Jesus have better uses for language
than that. Don't talk dirty or silly. That kind of talk
doesn't fit our style. Thanksgiving is our dialect.
EPHESIANS 5:3–4 MSG

An attitude of thanksgiving pushes out a lot of temptations,
including the temptation to gossip and backbite. It's all too easy
to complain about someone behind their back or to share a
juicy bit of gossip. But the Bible speaks sternly about careless
and unloving talk like this—and it shows us another way. When
our conversation is full of words of gratitude, we won't have
time for gossip and empty small talk. It may take time and
practice, but eventually we'll learn the dialect of thanksgiving
and no longer indulge in careless, hurtful conversations.

Whenever I begin to gossip or complain or engage in
thoughtless and silly words, remind me, Lord, that
You are calling me to learn a new language.

HOPE IN THE SIMPLE THINGS

"Go out and stand before me on the mountain," the LORD told him. And as Elijah stood there, the LORD passed by, and a mighty windstorm hit the mountain. It was such a terrible blast that the rocks were torn loose, but the LORD was not in the wind. After the wind there was an earthquake, but the LORD was not in the earthquake. And after the earthquake there was a fire, but the LORD was not in the fire. And after the fire there was the sound of a gentle whisper. When Elijah heard it, he wrapped his face in his cloak and went out and stood at the entrance of the cave. And a voice said, "What are you doing here, Elijah?"

1 KINGS 19:11–13 NLT

Sometimes when we're expecting or hoping for God to speak to us or act in an amazing and mighty way, He chooses to surprise us in a simple way instead—like in this story from 1 Kings, where God let Elijah experience a powerful wind and earthquake and fire. But then the way God chose to actually reveal Himself to Elijah was through the sound of a gentle whisper. Have hope and be listening for God in even the simplest things in your life.

Heavenly Father, help me not to miss how You are bringing me hope and healing in even the simplest, most unassuming ways. Amen.

Day 143

EVEN IF

The Lord is my light and the One Who saves me. Whom should I fear? The Lord is the strength of my life. Of whom should I be afraid? When sinful men, and all who hated me, came against me to destroy my flesh, they tripped and fell. Even if an army gathers against me, my heart will not be afraid. Even if war rises against me, I will be sure of You.

PSALM 27:1–3 NLV

Let this scripture give you strength and courage and inspire you to think of all kinds of "even if" statements to proclaim the hope God gives you, like these:

- "Even if the diagnosis isn't good, I trust You to take care of me and my family, God!"

- "Even if I don't get this job, I will trust You to provide for me, God!"

- "Even if this hardship doesn't go away, I know You will guide me as I endure it, God!"

- "Even if I make mistakes, I know You love and forgive me, God!"

Heavenly Father, thank You that no matter what uncertainties I face in life, I can be totally sure of You! Even if everything else falls apart, You never do— and I never will when I'm holding on to You. Amen.

PERFECT, ETERNAL GOD

*The counsel of the LORD standeth for ever,
the thoughts of his heart to all generations.*
PSALM 33:11 KJV

Our God isn't wishy-washy. He doesn't experience bad hair days or mood swings, nor is He swayed by trends, fads, or peer pressure. Our perfect, eternal God has no peer. From scripture, we can tell that God experiences emotions like love, grief, and pleasure. However, He isn't driven by His emotions as we sometimes are. That means we can trust God to be true to His promises, His plans, and His character—today, tomorrow, and always.

*Your great love is unfathomable, God! You know all
and still love me lavishly. Even when I fail, You see
me as who I am in Christ alone. Thank You, God!*

Day 145

PEACE RULES

And let the peace that comes from Christ rule in your hearts.
For as members of one body you are called to live in peace.
Colossians 3:15 nlt

Peace is a way of living our lives. It happens when we let Christ's peace into our lives to rule over our emotions, our doubts, and our worries, and then go one step more and let His peace control the way we live. Peace is God's gift of grace to us, but it is also the way to a graceful life, the path to harmony with the world around us.

Jesus, what an amazing gift of peace that comes from You.
Thank You for leading me on the path of a graceful life. Amen.

PRAISE THE CREATOR

O LORD, what a variety of things you have made! In wisdom you have made them all. The earth is full of your creatures.
PSALM 104:24 NLT

Whenever you get to spend time outside, whenever you do anything that makes you focus on and appreciate the natural world around you, remember to give praise to our Creator God! He has designed all of creation with incredible love and purpose. Every extraordinary detail of it reminds us in countless ways how awesome He is. The God who planned and created land and sky and sea and plants and animals certainly has great plans for men and women who are created in His image. Keep hoping in Him, seeking Him, and asking Him to show you His great plans for you.

Heavenly Father, just looking around outside fills me with great hope because Your creation is so meticulously designed and beautiful. I trust that You created me with beautiful plans too. Please show them to me in Your perfect timing. Amen.

Day 147

LET GOD REFRESH YOU

*If you pour yourself out for the hungry and satisfy the desire
of the afflicted, then shall your light rise in the darkness and
your gloom be as the noonday. And the LORD will guide you
continually and satisfy your desire in scorched places and
make your bones strong; and you shall be like a watered
garden, like a spring of water, whose waters do not fail.*

ISAIAH 58:10–11 ESV

Like a near-death plant we keep forgetting to water, sometimes we start to feel dry and ugly in our souls when we aren't
spending good time with God. We need to read His Word and
pray and worship Him so that He can lead and refresh us. He
can give the kind of living water that enables us never to feel
thirsty or dry again! In this passage, He says we are satisfied
and refreshed when we are pouring ourselves out to help
others in need. God is so good to continually fill us up so that
we always have plenty to share.

*Heavenly Father, please help me pour out my life in
service and care of others in exactly the ways You
want me to. As I do, thank You for refreshing me
with Your extraordinary living water! Amen.*

NOT ASHAMED

I am not ashamed of the gospel, because it is the power of God that brings salvation to everyone who believes.
ROMANS 1:16 NIV

Despite what the world might tell us, we have no reason to ever feel embarrassed or ashamed of believing in Jesus. Like Paul in the Bible, we should want to be able to say this—that we are not ashamed of the good news that Jesus came to earth to live a perfect life and teach us, died on the cross to pay for our sins, and then rose to life again and offers us eternal life too. When we share this good news and awesome hope with others, we help spread God's power to save people from their sins.

Heavenly Father, help me never to feel ashamed or embarrassed to share the good news about Jesus! Thank You for the true hope You give and for wanting to save all people from their sins! Amen.

LOOKING FORWARD

*I focus on this one thing: Forgetting the past
and looking forward to what lies ahead.*
PHILIPPIANS 3:13 NLT

As followers of Christ, we are people who look forward rather than backward. We have all made mistakes, but God does not want us to dwell on them or wallow in guilt and discouragement. Instead, He calls us to let go of the past, trusting Him to deal with it. His grace is new every moment.

Father, I sometimes ruminate over past mistakes. Help me not to wallow in the past. Instead, enable me to delight in Your grace, which is new each moment. Amen.

WATER THAT WELLS UP
TO ETERNAL LIFE

*Jesus, wearied as he was from his journey, was sitting beside
the well. . . . A woman from Samaria came to draw water.*
JOHN 4:6–7 ESV

Jesus said to the Samaritan woman at the well, "If you knew
the gift of God, and who it is that is saying to you, 'Give me a
drink,' you would have asked him, and he would have given you
living water" (John 4:10 ESV). The woman didn't understand.
She said to Jesus, "You have nothing to draw water with, and
the well is deep. Where do you get that living water?" (verse
11 ESV). Jesus told her, "Everyone who drinks of this water will
be thirsty again, but whoever drinks of the water that I will
give him will never be thirsty again. The water that I will give
him will become in him a spring of water welling up to eternal
life" (verses 13–14 ESV). So the woman said, "Sir, give me this
water" (verse 15 ESV).

*Dear Jesus, please help me to be like the woman at the
well. She trusted that You give the kind of water that makes
people never thirst again and leads to eternal life. I trust
and hope in You too—please quench and refresh me! Amen.*

Day 151

HOPE IN THE BEST BOSS

If your sinful old self is the boss over your mind, it leads to death. But if the Holy Spirit is the boss over your mind, it leads to life and peace. The mind that thinks only of ways to please the sinful old self is fighting against God. It is not able to obey God's Laws. It never can. Those who do what their sinful old selves want to do cannot please God. But you are not doing what your sinful old selves want you to do. You are doing what the Holy Spirit tells you to do, if you have God's Spirit living in you.

Romans 8:6–9 NLV

Before we trust in Jesus as Savior, our sin nature tells us what to do. And if we let sin be our boss, we are hopeless. We will regularly choose selfishness and greed; we will mostly be looking out for ourselves; and, in the end, we will destroy ourselves. But once we trust Jesus, we have His Holy Spirit living inside us—and He is the very best boss, who always wants the very best for us. He will lead us in a life of loving God and loving others and being filled with joy as we share the good news and spread hope for eternal life.

Heavenly Father, thank You for saving me and taking me from being a hopeless slave to sin to being a hopeful follower of the very best boss—Your Holy Spirit. Help me to choose to obey You every day! Amen.

LOVING SUPPORT

Let us think of ways to motivate one another
to acts of love and good works.
HEBREWS 10:24 NLT

Imagine that you're sitting in the bleachers watching one of your favorite young people play a sport. You jump up and cheer for him. You make sure he knows you're there by shouting out encouragement. Hearing your voice, he jumps higher and runs faster. That is the sort of excitement and support we need to show others around us. When we do all we can to encourage each other, love and good deeds will burst from us all.

Lord, help me to be a cheerleader for others. Help me to see
the world through their eyes and to say and do the things
I know would motivate and encourage them. Amen.

OPPORTUNITIES

*But I trusted in thee, O LORD: I said, Thou art
my God. My times are in thy hand.*
PSALM 31:14–15 KJV

Change can be exciting. It can also be uncomfortable, unwanted,
and—at times—even terrifying. If you're facing change and
find yourself feeling anxious or confused, turn to the God of
order and peace. He holds every twist and turn of your life in
His hands. Try looking at change through God's eyes, as an
opportunity for growth and an invitation to trust Him with
your deepest hopes and fears.

*Father, please give me spiritual eyes to see things
more like You see them. I want heaven's perspective
on situations and plans. Open my eyes, Lord!*

HOPE COMES FROM GOD

*Our hope comes from God. May He fill you with joy
and peace because of your trust in Him. May your
hope grow stronger by the power of the Holy Spirit.*
ROMANS 15:13 NLV

Think about the things you hope for. Do you have a long list?
How have you seen your hopes change with life and experience
and maturity? The reason we have any hope for good things at
all is because God is the giver of hope. Every good and perfect
gift comes from Him, James 1:17 tells us. And our ultimate, final
hope is in the promise of heaven where there will be no more
sickness, sadness, or pain—only perfect paradise forever as
God dwells with us. With each new day, let your hope in God
and His good gifts grow stronger and stronger by the power
of the Holy Spirit in you.

*Heavenly Father, thank You for giving me hope. All gifts
and good things come from You, and I trust that You
have good plans for me here on earth and a perfect
forever waiting for me in heaven with You. Amen.*

A BROKEN PROMISE

Peter replied, "Even if all fall away on account of you, I never will." "Truly I tell you," Jesus answered, "this very night, before the rooster crows, you will disown me three times." But Peter declared, "Even if I have to die with you, I will never disown you."
MATTHEW 26:33–35 NIV

Have you ever broken a promise and felt helpless to regain trust and mend the relationship? There is hope even then. Remember, for example, Peter's big broken promise to Jesus. He had told Jesus that there was no way he would ever deny knowing Him. It was unthinkable to Peter. But then when Jesus was captured and taken to be killed, Peter did deny Jesus, just like Jesus had warned. Afterward, Peter felt awful and bitterly ashamed of himself (Matthew 26:69–75). Still, Jesus loved and forgave Peter—and Peter went on to do great things to spread the news of Jesus. Jesus loves and forgives us and never wants to hold our sins against us when we confess and repent.

Dear Jesus, help me to remember that even though Peter messed up big-time, there was still hope. There's hope for me too when I break promises and make mistakes. Remind me how You love to forgive. Amen.

TEN PERCENT

The earth is the LORD's, and everything in it.
PSALM 24:1 NLT

Do you tithe? Giving 10 percent of your income specifically to God's work is a good discipline. But sometimes we act as though that 10 percent is God's and the other 90 percent is ours. We forget that everything is God's. Through grace, He shares all of creation with us. When we look at it that way, our 10 percent tithe seems a little stingy!

Heavenly Father, everything belongs to You—even the cattle on a thousand hills. Thank You for sharing Your wealth with me. Help me to share it lavishly with others. Amen.

AN ENDURING FOUNDATION

With praise and thanksgiving they sang to the LORD:
"He is good; his love toward Israel endures forever."
And all the people gave a great shout of praise to the LORD,
because the foundation of the house of the LORD was laid.
EZRA 3:11 NIV

What do you consider the foundation of your life to be? We all rely on different things—family, friends, money, careers, our homes—and while these things aren't bad in themselves, none of them will endure. Family and friends will die, money comes and goes, careers come to an end, homes are temporary shelters. Only God is a firm foundation that endures forever. When we rely on Him as the foundation that underlies all the other aspects of our lives, then we can go through life with a sense of joyful gratitude. Our home will be His unchanging presence.

My heart and soul shout for joy to You, oh Lord,
the foundation of my life, for Your love endures forever.

THE HEALING OF THE CENTURION'S SERVANT

When he had entered Capernaum, a centurion came forward to him, appealing to him, "Lord, my servant is lying paralyzed at home, suffering terribly." And he said to him, "I will come and heal him." But the centurion replied, "Lord, I am not worthy to have you come under my roof, but only say the word, and my servant will be healed. For I too am a man under authority, with soldiers under me. And I say to one, 'Go,' and he goes, and to another, 'Come,' and he comes, and to my servant, 'Do this,' and he does it." When Jesus heard this, he marveled and said to those who followed him, "Truly, I tell you, with no one in Israel have I found such faith."

MATTHEW 8:5–10 ESV

This army captain had such great faith in Jesus, he didn't even ask Jesus to come back to his house to heal his servant. He was humble, and he trusted that Jesus could just say the word from anywhere and his servant would be healed. And the captain was absolutely right! "Jesus said, 'Go; let it be done for you as you have believed.' And the servant was healed at that very moment" (Matthew 8:13 ESV).

Heavenly Father, I want to have faith like this army captain. Help me to trust that You can simply say the word and absolutely anything can happen! Amen.

Day 159

CONFIDENTLY TRUST THE LORD

How joyful are those who fear the LORD and delight in obeying his commands. Their children will be successful everywhere; an entire generation of godly people will be blessed. They themselves will be wealthy, and their good deeds will last forever. Light shines in the darkness for the godly. They are generous, compassionate, and righteous. Good comes to those who lend money generously and conduct their business fairly. Such people will not be overcome by evil. Those who are righteous will be long remembered. They do not fear bad news; they confidently trust the LORD to care for them.

PSALM 112:1–7 NLT

Those of us who fear the Lord have such great hope for both this life and the life to come. God wants to bless us both now and eternally for loving and following Him.

Heavenly Father, thank You for the promises in this psalm. I confidently trust that You care for me and want to bless me in amazing ways as I put all my hope in You! Amen.

TRANSFORMED

And Sarah declared, "God has brought me laughter.
All who hear about this will laugh with me."
GENESIS 21:6 NLT

The first time we read of Sarah laughing, it was because she doubted God. She didn't believe that at her age she would have a baby. But God didn't hold her laughter against her. Instead, He transformed it. He turned her laughter of scorn and doubt into the laughter of fulfillment and grace.

Father Redeemer, thank You for taking my very worst
moments and transforming them into a story You
can use for Your purpose and Your glory. Amen.

ALL PEOPLE!

I urge, then, first of all, that petitions, prayers, intercession and thanksgiving be made for all people.
1 TIMOTHY 2:1 NIV

Most of us can think of at least one individual in our life who is difficult to like. The Bible never says we have to like everybody, but it does say we need to pray for everyone—even those people who are so hard to put up with. It's one thing, though, to pray for these individuals, asking God to help them and bless them. But the Bible goes one step further and says we are also to be *thankful* for these people. That may seem like a real challenge when it comes to some people. How can we be thankful for people who get on our nerves? And what about people who are cruel or lack integrity? The Bible doesn't give us any wiggle room here, though. As we form a habit of praying and thanking God for *all people*, we may find we begin to see them differently.

Lord, I ask that You be with the individuals I find difficult to like. Bless them. Heal them. Strengthen them in Your love. Thank You for making these people. Help me to see them with Your eyes.

Day 162

HOPE IN THE MIDST OF TRIAL

Don't be surprised at the fiery trials you are going through,
as if something strange were happening to you. Instead,
be very glad—for these trials make you partners with Christ
in his suffering, so that you will have the wonderful joy
of seeing his glory when it is revealed to all the world.
1 PETER 4:12–13 NLT

You can have hope in the midst of hardship when you remember that your trials don't take God by surprise—and as hard as they are, your trials don't need to take you by surprise either. Jesus said, "Here on earth you will have many trials and sorrows. But take heart, because I have overcome the world" (John 16:33 NLT). God is sovereign over your current trial. He can rescue you at any moment, and He will in His perfect timing. Until then, trust that He sustains you and comforts you; He never leaves you. Scripture says you become partners with Him in His suffering as you endure your trial. Let Him use the time of suffering to bond you ever stronger and closer to Him—and one day you will share in the wonderful joy of seeing His glory revealed to all the world.

Dear Jesus, please draw me closer to You in the midst of
this trial. Help me to endure and learn and grow in the
ways You want me to. I trust You are sovereign and good
and that none of this takes you by surprise. Amen.

ALL CIRCUMSTANCES

*Give thanks in all circumstances; for this is
God's will for you in Christ Jesus.*
1 THESSALONIANS 5:18 NIV

We are used to thinking of thankfulness as something we feel
only in circumstances we label as "good." We thank God for a
loved one's healing, for a salary raise, or for the birth of a child.
We are less likely to feel gratitude at the death of a loved one,
the loss of a job, or a chronic illness that just won't go away.
But the Bible tells us to give thanks in *all* circumstances. This
doesn't mean we're expected to feel happy about hard or tragic
events. God doesn't ask us to deny our sorrow, anger, or dis-
appointment. But even in the midst of those feelings, we can
choose to say "thank You" to God, knowing that, even now, He
is working in our lives.

Help me, Jesus, to say "thank You" even when it's hard.

OPEN TO JOY

"The joy of the LORD is your strength."
NEHEMIAH 8:10 NIV

Our God is a God of joy. He is not a God of sighing and gloom. Open yourself to His joy. It is a gift of grace He longs to give you. He knows it will make you strong.

Oh Lord, giver of joy and source of my strength,
thank You for these gifts that are mine in abundance.
Help me to rely on Your joy and strength. Amen.

Day 165

THE TRUE YOU

Examine me, O LORD, and prove me;
try my reins and my heart.
PSALM 26:2 KJV

Some women spend a great amount of time trying to look beautiful on the outside, while paying little attention to what's on the inside. God's words and His Spirit can help reveal the true you, from the inside out. Ask God where your character needs some touching up—or perhaps a total makeover. See if your thoughts, your words, and your actions line up with the woman you'd like to see smiling back at you in the mirror each morning.

Search me, O God, and know my heart.
Show me anything that is blocking my relationship
with You. Restore me to Your heart, Lord.

TRUE EQUALITY

For in Christ Jesus you are all sons of God, through faith. For as many of you as were baptized into Christ have put on Christ. There is neither Jew nor Greek, there is neither slave nor free, there is no male and female, for you are all one in Christ Jesus.
GALATIANS 3:26–28 ESV

Is there any hope for equality in our world? Yes—and Jesus alone offers true equality. Because of sin in the world, people will never get equality exactly right. There will always be evil ideologies spreading the lie that certain groups of people are better than others. But in God's eyes, because of Jesus, every single person is the same in value. We are all so loved by God that He sent Jesus to die to save us from our sins. And when we humbles ourselves, repent of sin, and trust in Jesus, we become children of the one true God—the King of all kings. That makes us all equally royal!

Heavenly Father, thank You that anyone can be Your child by trusting that only Jesus saves. You offer the only true equality through Him. Help me to share with others the awesome truth that we all have equal standing with You. Amen.

HOPE IN THE GOOD SHEPHERD

"I am the good shepherd. The good shepherd lays down his life for the sheep. The hired hand is not the shepherd and does not own the sheep. So when he sees the wolf coming, he abandons the sheep and runs away. Then the wolf attacks the flock and scatters it. The man runs away because he is a hired hand and cares nothing for the sheep. I am the good shepherd; I know my sheep and my sheep know me—just as the Father knows me and I know the Father—and I lay down my life for the sheep."

JOHN 10:11–15 NIV

Jesus said He is the good shepherd, and then later He proved it by giving up His own life to save others from sin. Anyone who trusts in Jesus as Savior becomes a sheep under Jesus' care—and that's a wonderful creature to be, a wonderful place to be. Think of the specific ways you have seen His care and guidance, and trust that He will never stop loving and shepherding you.

Dear Jesus, thank You for letting me be Your sheep. I want to be guided and cared for by You forever! Amen.

HE WILL NOT STOP HELPING YOU

David said to his son Solomon, "Be strong. Have strength of heart, and do it. Do not be afraid or troubled, for the Lord God, my God, is with you. He will not stop helping you. He will not leave you until all the work of the house of the Lord is finished."
1 CHRONICLES 28:20 NLV

When you're facing a challenge or a lot of hard work that feels overwhelming and stirs up fear and anxiety, sometimes you just need a little pep talk like Solomon got from his dad. Do you have people in your life who give you good pep talks? Thank them for their encouragement and thank God for blessing you with their presence in your life. Other times you just need to remember scriptures like this and let God's Word give you the exact pep talk you need, like "Be strong and brave, and just do it! Don't be afraid, because God is with you! He won't stop helping you; He will never leave you!"

Heavenly Father, thank You for the people who give me good pep talks and also for all the pep talks I need that come from Your Word! Help me to remember them exactly when I need them. Amen.

NEW EVERY MORNING

But this I call to mind, and therefore I have hope:
The steadfast love of the LORD never ceases; his mercies
never come to an end; they are new every morning;
great is your faithfulness. "The LORD is my portion,"
says my soul, "therefore I will hope in him."
LAMENTATIONS 3:21–24 ESV

As you wake up to a new day, hopefully you've had a good night's rest and feel like you have a fresh start, no matter what happened yesterday. God's Word talks about how God's love and mercy are new to us every morning. On good mornings and on those not-so-good mornings, as you open your eyes and climb out of bed, reflect on this scripture and let it give you courage and hope for whatever you're facing that day.

Heavenly Father, thank You for brand-new days
that offer a fresh start. I hope in You and Your great
faithfulness, love, and mercy today! Amen.

ACCORDING TO YOUR FAITH

*As Jesus went on from there, two blind men followed him,
calling out, "Have mercy on us, Son of David!" When he had
gone indoors, the blind men came to him, and he asked them,
"Do you believe that I am able to do this?" "Yes, Lord," they
replied. Then he touched their eyes and said, "According to
your faith let it be done to you"; and their sight was restored.*
MATTHEW 9:27–30 NIV

When you ask God for something in prayer, think of this passage of scripture where Jesus healed two blind men, restoring their sight. Tell Jesus what you need and then picture Him asking you, "Do you believe that I am able to do this?" Answer Him, "Yes, Lord!" and mean it. Tell Him you know without a doubt that He is able to do it. Then trust Him to answer your prayer according to His perfect will, His perfect timing, and His perfect plans.

*Dear Jesus, I have hope and faith that You can do
anything! Nothing I ask of You is ever too hard for
You! Let Your will be done. I praise You! Amen.*

BECAUSE OF HIS GREATNESS

It is God Who sits on the throne above the earth. The people living on the earth are like grasshoppers. He spreads out the heavens like a curtain. . . . It is He Who brings rulers down to nothing. He makes the judges of the earth as nothing. . . . Lift up your eyes and see. Who has made these stars? It is the One Who leads them out by number. He calls them all by name. Because of the greatness of His strength, and because He is strong in power, not one of them is missing.

ISAIAH 40:22–23, 26 NLV

How does being compared to just a grasshopper give us any hope? Because it reminds us of God's awesome greatness. He spread out the skies as easily as if they were curtains. He is able to defeat any human power or scheme. He made the stars and counts them and even has a name for each of them. And this same amazing God knows and cares about every single detail of each one of us too! We are so small compared to God, yet we are dearly loved and perfectly cared for by His almighty hand.

Heavenly Father, You fill me with such hope and courage because I know You are so much bigger than me and anything in this world—and You are always taking care of me. Thank You! Amen.

HOPE IN A DIFFICULT WORKPLACE

*Whatever you do, work at it with all your heart,
as working for the Lord, not for human masters, since
you know that you will receive an inheritance from the
Lord as a reward. It is the Lord Christ you are serving.*
Colossians 3:23–24 niv

In a hopeless-seeming work situation, let God help you find joy and purpose in the work anyway. What is your attitude like at work? How could it change if you applied this scripture from Colossians to it? (Look up and apply Philippians 2:13–15 to your attitude too!) No matter what kind of work situation you're in, picture God as your boss overseeing you. He's your heavenly Father and the very best leader. He loves you more than anyone ever, and He blesses and rewards good work like no one else can. So do all your work with all your heart! Let God teach you and grow you and give you joy through everything—even when it feels hard and hopeless. He will either change your attitude or change your situation as you trust Him to guide you and care for you.

Heavenly Father, please help me with my work when it feels hopeless and unbearable. Please either change my attitude so I can have joy or change my work situation. Either way, I trust that You never stop helping me and loving me. I want to do all things for Your glory! Amen.

JESUS IS THE RESURRECTION AND THE LIFE

Jesus called in a loud voice, "Lazarus, come out!" The dead man came out.
JOHN 11:43–44 NIV

As shown in the miraculous account of the resurrection of Lazarus from the dead, Jesus had all power to heal and raise the dead to life and still does today—according to His will and to help people believe in Him—through the Holy Spirit. But when He doesn't choose to heal in this life, don't forget Martha and Jesus' exchange from earlier in this same passage of scripture:

"Lord," Martha said to Jesus, "if you had been here, my brother would not have died. But I know that even now God will give you whatever you ask." Jesus said to her, "Your brother will rise again." Martha answered, "I know he will rise again in the resurrection at the last day." Jesus said to her, "I am the resurrection and the life. The one who believes in me will live, even though they die; and whoever lives by believing in me will never die. Do you believe this?" (John 11:21–26 NIV).

Heavenly Father, I trust Your ability to heal and raise the dead to life. I know You have power to do so at any time, in any place. Ultimately, I believe with all my heart that You raise to eternal life everyone who believes in You as Savior. Amen.

THE HOLY SPIRIT

*Be filled with the Holy Spirit, singing psalms and hymns
and spiritual songs among yourselves, and making music
to the Lord in your hearts. And give thanks for everything
to God the Father in the name of our Lord Jesus Christ.*
EPHESIANS 5:18–20 NLT

When we choose to practice gratitude, we invite the Holy
Spirit into our lives. As we sing out our thanks, both together
in community and alone as individuals, we are making room
in our hearts for the Spirit to fill us. The Spirit, in turn, brings
a sense of peace and joy that underlies even the hard things
in our lives. Filled with the Holy Spirit, we find that gratitude
becomes easier to practice. But it all begins with our choice—
to practice thanksgiving instead of worry, to praise instead of
complain, and to sing instead of curse.

*Teach me, faithful friend, to give thanks
always and for everything.*

MISUNDERSTOOD

Let my sentence come forth from thy presence;
let thine eyes behold the things that are equal.
PSALM 17:2 KJV

Not everyone will understand the unseen story behind what you say and do. There will be times when you're misunderstood, slandered, or even rejected. This is when your true character shines through. How you respond to adversity and unfair accusations says a lot about you and the God you serve. Ask God to help you address any blind spots you may have about your own character. Treat your critics with respect. Then move ahead with both confidence and humility.

God, it hurts when I'm misunderstood and judged.
I give my heart to You for healing and understanding.
Help me treat others with respect and grace.

GOD OF THE WEATHER

*"God's voice is glorious in the thunder. We can't even
imagine the greatness of his power. He directs the snow
to fall on the earth and tells the rain to pour down.
Then everyone stops working so they can watch his power."*
JOB 37:5–7 NLT

Scientists today can make all kinds of smart predictions about
the weather and climate change, but no one can control it
except the one who created it—our extraordinary God! Let the
weather fill you with greater awe and respect for Him. Bow
before Him in humility and ask for His protection, provision,
and care. Thank Him when the weather blesses you, and choose
to trust and praise Him even when it doesn't—because you
know you are a child of the powerful King who commands it,
who uses it any way He chooses to work out His perfect plans.

*Heavenly Father, my hope is not in this world or in any
brilliant person who makes predictions or plans here.
No one is sovereign like You are! You are awesome
and mighty and in control of all things. Amen.*

THE LORD—YOUR STRENGTH AND ROCK

I love you, O LORD, my strength. The LORD is my rock and my fortress and my deliverer, my God, my rock, in whom I take refuge, my shield, and the horn of my salvation, my stronghold. I call upon the LORD, who is worthy to be praised, and I am saved from my enemies.

PSALM 18:1–3 ESV

Anytime something in your life feels shaky—maybe your family or relationships are going through trouble, or you're suffering from a job loss, or health problems are scaring you or a loved one—remember that the Lord is your rock-solid source of strength and stability. He promises that you will not be shaken. Yes, things in your life might tremble and quake at times, but ultimately, no matter what happens, God keeps you safe and secure.

Heavenly Father, You are strong and steady all the time— in every place I am and in every problem I experience. When things feel shaky in my life, please remind me to keep my feet planted firmly on You, my solid rock. Amen.

GOD TURNS MOURNING INTO DANCING

*"Hear me, LORD, and have mercy on me. Help me, O LORD."
You have turned my mourning into joyful dancing.
You have taken away my clothes of mourning and clothed
me with joy, that I might sing praises to you and not be
silent. O LORD my God, I will give you thanks forever!*
PSALM 30:10–12 NLT

Only our awesome, loving God can take any kind of grief, anxiety, sorrow, or pain in our lives and turn it into such joy that we feel like dancing. He might do that for us here on earth in certain ways, or we might have to wait until heaven—but we can trust that He will. With every hard thing you might go through, you have a choice either to pull away from God or to cling more tightly to Him. The first choice will only bring despair, but the second choice will lead to dancing!

*Heavenly Father, I want to get closer to You in the midst
of hardship and pain. I trust that You will turn every
sorrow into total joy and dancing someday. Amen.*

Day 179

AMAZING EXPECTATIONS

*Listen to my voice in the morning, Lord. Each morning
I bring my requests to you and wait expectantly.*
PSALM 5:3 NLT

You need to get in the habit of hoping. Instead of getting up in the morning and sighing as you face another dreary day, practice saying hello to God as soon as you wake up. Listen for what He wants to say to your heart. Expect Him to do amazing things each day.

*Good morning, Lord. I can easily forget how necessary it
is to begin my day in sweet communion with You. Tune my
heart's ear to the lovely sound of Your voice. Amen.*

THE SPIRIT INTERCEDES

Likewise the Spirit helps us in our weakness. For we do not know what to pray for as we ought, but the Spirit himself intercedes for us with groanings too deep for words. And he who searches hearts knows what is the mind of the Spirit, because the Spirit intercedes for the saints according to the will of God.
ROMANS 8:26–27 ESV

Sometimes you might feel so hopeless, so scared and worried, that you don't have the slightest clue how to pray. That's when you must remember you have the Holy Spirit in you, who actually prays for you when you can't find the words. Incredible! Thank God for that blessing and let it fill you with hope and courage. God never leaves you. He always knows everything you think and everything you need. He helps you even when you don't know how to ask for help!

Heavenly Father, thank You for Your Holy Spirit who acts as my helper and even prays for me when I don't know how. Thank You for knowing me better than I know myself! Amen.

LEARN FROM THE PRODIGAL SON

"He arose and came to his father. But while he was still a long way off, his father saw him and felt compassion, and ran and embraced him and kissed him. And the son said to him, 'Father, I have sinned against heaven and before you. I am no longer worthy to be called your son.' But the father said to his servants, 'Bring quickly the best robe, and put it on him, and put a ring on his hand, and shoes on his feet. And bring the fattened calf and kill it, and let us eat and celebrate. For this my son was dead, and is alive again; he was lost, and is found.' And they began to celebrate."

LUKE 15:20–24 ESV

If you ever feel like you've messed up so much that you might never be forgiven, like you need to run away from a relationship or situation and never, ever come back—then think of the story Jesus told of the foolish son to help you remember that God loves you dearly *no matter what.* Just as the father in the story welcomed back his son who had made bad choices—with extravagant love and even a huge celebration—God, your heavenly Father, will welcome you back when you turn away from your sin and run into His open arms.

Heavenly Father, I can't thank You enough for Your endless love for me. In Your mercy, please lead me out of sinful patterns and mistakes and into Your truth and wisdom. Amen.

UNTIL THE VERY LAST MOMENTS

*One of the criminals who were hanged railed at him, saying,
"Are you not the Christ? Save yourself and us!" But the other
rebuked him, saying, "Do you not fear God, since you are under
the same sentence of condemnation? And we indeed justly,
for we are receiving the due reward of our deeds; but this
man has done nothing wrong." And he said, "Jesus, remember
me when you come into your kingdom." And he said to him,
"Truly, I say to you, today you will be with me in paradise."*
LUKE 23:39–43 ESV

Jesus gives grace until even the very last moments of life,
wanting everyone to believe in Him and receive Him as Savior.
If you have friends and loved ones who are not yet believers,
keep on hoping for them, praying for them, and sharing God's
great love with them. Jesus wants to give them every chance
possible for eternal life in paradise.

*Dear Jesus, thank You for the example of the criminal
beside You who believed at the last moment. It gives me
so much hope for people I know who don't yet trust in You.
Please humble them and soften their hearts to You! Amen.*

Day 183

A LOVELY PLACE

How lovely is your dwelling place, Lord Almighty!
Psalm 84:1 niv

Imagine this: God considers your heart His home! It's the place where He dwells. And as a result, your heart is a lovely place, filled with the grace of the almighty God.

O Lord Almighty, I humbly invite You into my heart's home. Fill it with Your loveliness so that I can experience the comfort of Your presence and Your peace. Amen.

COURAGE AND CLEVERNESS

When she could hide him no longer, she got a papyrus basket for him and coated it with tar and pitch. Then she placed the child in it and put it among the reeds along the bank of the Nile. His sister stood at a distance to see what would happen to him.
EXODUS 2:3–4 NIV

One of the Israelite babies saved from Pharaoh's evil plan was Moses, and his mother was Jochebed. When it became too difficult to keep hiding and protecting baby Moses as he grew, Jochebed showed courage and clever thinking. She came up with a plan to put Moses in a basket in the river near where Pharaoh's daughter liked to bathe. Jochebed hoped the princess would find Moses and adopt him as her own. And that's exactly what happened. Moses was safe and could grow up to be the great leader God planned for him to be!

Heavenly Father, please help me to have hope and courage like Jochebed. Give me clever ideas when I need them to help carry out Your perfect plans. Amen.

MORE THAN MOTHERLY LOVE

That our sons may be as plants grown up in their youth; that our daughters may be as corner stones, polished after the similitude of a palace.

PSALM 144:12 KJV

Good food, a good night's sleep, a good education, a good home that's safe and overflowing with love. . . Good mothers try to provide what their children need. But children need more. Like adults, children have spiritual needs as well as physical and emotional ones. That's why praying for your children every day is more than just a good idea. It's a reminder that your children need more than motherly love. They also need their heavenly Father's involvement in their lives.

Father, I offer up my children to Your loving care. Help me care for them and love them well, but show them where my love comes from. Reveal Yourself to them individually.

THE LORD LIGHTS THE DARKNESS

*You make my lamp bright. The Lord
my God lights my darkness.*
PSALM 18:28 NLV

The darkness of hopelessness can be frighteningly deep—but it is never so deep that God cannot shine His light into it. In fact, the deeper the darkness, the brighter God's light in contrast. The darkness can never overcome it. If you find yourself wandering in darkness, with only more darkness in your view ahead, have you turned away from God's light? Sometimes circumstances that are no fault of our own drop us into the darkness of hopelessness; and sometimes our own willful choosing lands us there. But God's light never stops shining to guide us. We have to look for it and follow it. How? God can reveal His light in any way He chooses. Often He does so through our regular time in the truth of His Word, through moments of worship and prayer, and through fellowship with other believers.

*Heavenly Father, when I find myself in darkness,
please light it up as only You can. I always
want to look for and follow You! Amen.*

THEY FEARED GOD

The king of Egypt said to the Hebrew midwives, whose names were Shiphrah and Puah, "When you are helping the Hebrew women during childbirth on the delivery stool, if you see that the baby is a boy, kill him; but if it is a girl, let her live." The midwives, however, feared God and did not do what the king of Egypt had told them to do; they let the boys live.

EXODUS 1:15–17 NIV

The Hebrew midwives were told to kill the Hebrew baby boys, but they would not do it. Why? Because they "feared God." They respected Him and knew He was greater than any earthly power. They trusted that if they did the right thing—refusing to kill innocent babies—God would protect and bless them. And they were exactly right. Scripture goes on to say, "God was kind to the midwives and the people increased and became even more numerous. And because the midwives feared God, he gave them families of their own" (Exodus 1:20–21 NIV).

Almighty God, I respect and trust and hope in You far more than any earthly power or authority. Help me to always do what is right in Your eyes. Amen.

FREE!

For the Lord is the Spirit, and wherever the Spirit of the Lord is, there is freedom.

2 Corinthians 3:17 nlt

How do you know when the Holy Spirit is present in your life? You should be able to tell by the sense of freedom you feel. If you feel oppressed, obsessed, or depressed, something in your life is out of kilter. Seek out God's Spirit. He wants you to be free.

Holy Spirit, fill me with a sense of freedom only You can provide. Free my spirit from chains of oppression, and draw me into the wide-open spaces of Your peace. Amen.

Day 189

HAND IN HAND

*Let the peace that comes from Christ rule in your
hearts. For as members of one body you are called
to live in peace. And always be thankful.*
Colossians 3:15 nlt

Paul, the author of this scripture passage, is letting us in on a
secret here. The peace that comes from Christ, the peace that
passes all human understanding, is connected to thankfulness. The more we thank God for everything, both the lovely
things and the hard things, the lovable people and the not-so-
lovable ones, the more we will experience the peace of Christ.
Gratitude is an effective tool for sweeping the anxiety out of
our hearts. Complaining and feeling dissatisfied—behaviors
that are the opposite of thankfulness—lead to anxiety, stress,
and resentment. But peace and gratitude go hand in hand.

*Lord, help me to form a habit of thankfulness.
I want to live in Your peace.*

GOD WILL GUIDE

By day the L ORD went ahead of them in a pillar of cloud to guide them on their way and by night in a pillar of fire to give them light, so that they could travel by day or night. Neither the pillar of cloud by day nor the pillar of fire by night left its place in front of the people.
E XODUS 13:21–22 NIV

Sometimes we hope and pray for God to guide us with the same kind of impossible-to-miss signs in the sky that he gave the Israelites in the wilderness. But even if His guidance is not quite so clear and obvious, He will lead us just the same when we are devoted to Him. His Word promises it: "Trust in the L ORD with all your heart and lean not on your own understanding; in all your ways submit to him, and he will make your paths straight" (Proverbs 3:5–6 NIV).

Dear Lord, please lead and guide me and make my paths straight. Help me not to miss the signs and directions You are giving me. I trust You, and I submit my ways to You. Amen.

EXTRAORDINARY ENDURANCE

*We have this treasure in jars of clay to show that this
all-surpassing power is from God and not from us.
We are hard pressed on every side, but not crushed;
perplexed, but not in despair; persecuted, but not
abandoned; struck down, but not destroyed.*

2 CORINTHIANS 4:7–9 NIV

In what ways are you feeling hard pressed on every side today?
Perplexed? Persecuted? Struck down? You might feel like
you can't bear another second of the hardship you are going
through, but trust this scripture. No matter what's happening,
you will *not* be crushed. You will *not* fall into despair. You will
never be abandoned. You will *never* be destroyed. God will help
you have extraordinary endurance. He will give you just enough
fresh strength and energy and hope and joy at just the right
moments. Hang in there with faith and confidence in the one
true almighty God! You can trust His Word and His promises.

*Heavenly Father, when I feel like I'm at my
breaking point, remind me You'll never let that
happen. You are sovereign and good! You give me
supernatural strength, endurance, hope, and joy!*

JESUS' REPRESENTATIVE

*And whatever you do or say, do it as a representative of the
Lord Jesus, giving thanks through him to God the Father.*
COLOSSIANS 3:17 NLT

Making a conscious effort to act and speak the way Jesus would
radically changes the way we live our lives. It's not easy. It
takes practice and attention. But one way to make it easier is
to build the habit of thanking Jesus for being with us moment
by moment. Sometimes we may not be able to sense His presence—but thanking Him anyway, regardless of our perceptions,
builds our confidence. It helps us to stay on track. We have
a greater sense of His companionship with us through all of
our lives' challenges and joys. He walks with us and guides our
choices so that we can be good representatives of His love.

*I want to be Your representative, Lord Jesus.
Thank You that You are always with me.*

SIT AT THE LORD'S FEET

*A woman named Martha welcomed [Jesus] into her
house. And she had a sister called Mary, who sat
at the Lord's feet and listened to his teaching.*
LUKE 10:38–39 ESV

When you're feeling hopelessly unproductive, as if you never quite get enough accomplished, remember the story of Mary and Martha. They were two sisters who were excited to welcome Jesus into their home. Martha excelled at hosting and tending to all the details of good hospitality. But Martha grew very frustrated with Mary because when Jesus arrived, Mary didn't help her with all those detailed tasks. Mary simply sat at Jesus' feet to listen to everything He had to say. Both sisters loved Jesus and were showing it in their own ways. But Jesus lovingly told Martha that Mary had chosen what was best, urging her not to fuss so much over the work to be done but to simply enjoy His company and listen to His teaching.

*Dear Jesus, I want to show my love to You by the good
works I can do, like Martha, but I also want to choose the
best way by enjoying simply being with You, like Mary.
Please help me take time to choose what is best. Amen.*

THE ONE WHO LIFTS YOUR HEAD

*Many are saying of me, "There is no help for him in
God." But You, O Lord, are a covering around me, my
shining-greatness, and the One Who lifts my head.
I was crying to the Lord with my voice. And He answered
me from His holy mountain. I lay down and slept,
and I woke up again, for the Lord keeps me safe.*
PSALM 3:2–5 NLV

Sometimes life feels so painful or depressing or frustrating or
scary or lonely that you just need to go to bed and cry your
eyes out. And that's okay! As you do, think of God comforting
you, envisioning Him, like this scripture says, as the covering
around you. He is the one who helps you and gives you "shining-
greatness" again. He lifts your head and wants to help you get
out of bed and face the hard things going on. Crying out to
God, pouring out all your feelings to Him, can be incredibly
beneficial, but then remember to let Him lovingly lift your
head and help you!

*Heavenly Father, I'm so grateful You let me cry
everything out to You. And then You lift my head
again with loving care. I can face anything with You
as my constant source of help and hope. Amen.*

FOR ETERNITY

My health may fail, and my spirit may grow weak, but God remains the strength of my heart; he is mine forever.
PSALM 73:26 NLT

Sooner or later, our bodies let us down. Even the healthiest of us will one day have to face old age. When our bodies' strength fails us, we may feel discouraged and depressed. But even then, we can find joy and strength in our God. When our hearts belong to the Creator of the universe, we realize we are far more than our bodies. Because of God's unfailing grace, we will be truly healthy for all eternity.

God, when I feel discouraged by aches and pains that bring me down, help me to remember that my life here on earth is barely a breath in the scope of eternity. Amen.

GOD SENT HIS ANGEL

The king declared to Daniel, "O Daniel, servant of the living God, has your God, whom you serve continually, been able to deliver you from the lions?" Then Daniel said to the king, "O king, live forever! My God sent his angel and shut the lions' mouths, and they have not harmed me, because I was found blameless before him."

DANIEL 6:20–22 ESV

God could have made Daniel fly out of the den. He could have killed the lions. He could have made the king switch places with Daniel. He could have saved Daniel in any way He chose. But God sent His angel to shut the mouths of the lions. God can send his angels to help and rescue you too at any moment for any reason, in ways you may never even realize.

Heavenly Father, You have angels You can send to help me anywhere, anytime. Remembering Your host of angels gives me hope and courage to face any problem or challenge or danger or fear that might come my way. Amen.

A CHILDLIKE FAITH

*Lo, children are an heritage of the LORD:
and the fruit of the womb is his reward.*
PSALM 127:3 KJV

A child is a gift that is literally heaven-sent. You don't have to have children of your own to care about the kids around you—or to learn from them. In the New Testament, Jesus talks about how our faith should resemble that of a child's. To understand why, consider this: children believe what they hear, love unconditionally, and say what they think. What a wonderful way to relate to God.

Father, breathe new life into my faith. I want to trust You and enjoy You with the same delight and wonder that a child has for life.

LET TROUBLE BUILD YOUR HOPE

*We are glad for our troubles also. We know that troubles
help us learn not to give up. When we have learned not
to give up, it shows we have stood the test. When we
have stood the test, it gives us hope. Hope never makes
us ashamed because the love of God has come into our
hearts through the Holy Spirit Who was given to us.*
ROMANS 5:3–5 NLV

We never need to go asking for trouble; somehow it manages to
find us all on its own. What trouble has come your way lately?
Can you let Romans 5 help you think about it in a healthy,
positive way? We can be glad about trouble by remembering
that it helps us learn not to give up and strengthens our hope
that things will be better in the future. When our hope is in
the right place—in the almighty God who has saved us through
His Son and given us His Holy Spirit now and perfect life in
heaven in the future—we will never be ashamed or defeated.
Just as God sent His Son to save us at exactly the right time,
He will deliver us out of any trouble at exactly the right time.

*Heavenly Father, help me not to run away from trouble
but rather face it with Your power in me. You use
trouble in my life to help me learn to not give up and to
depend on You. You have saved me through Your Son,
and You are my ultimate hope and peace. Amen.*

HOPE FROM THE PAST

Then Moses said to the people, "Remember this day in which you came out from Egypt, out of the house of slavery, for by a strong hand the LORD brought you out from this place."
EXODUS 13:3 ESV

Sometimes we just want to forget hardship and loss and pain because they were awful and we're so glad they're in the past. Yet in some ways, remembering them can give us great hope. We must never forget how God helped us through them or rescued us from them. Looking back and remembering grows our faith and trust that God will help and rescue again in the future. Moses told the people of Israel to remember the amazing day that God finally brought them out of slavery in Egypt. Just as they did, we too need to remember the times God has rescued us from trials and tribulations.

Heavenly Father, every bit of help and rescue I have ever received has ultimately come from You! I don't want to forget! Build my faith and hope in You as I recall even the hardest things in the past and remember how You carried me through. Amen.

AN EVERLASTING CROWN

Do you not know that in a race all the runners run, but only one gets the prize? Run in such a way as to get the prize. Everyone who competes in the games goes into strict training. They do it to get a crown that will not last, but we do it to get a crown that will last forever.
1 CORINTHIANS 9:24–25 NIV

How we run our race here on earth, on the path God has mapped out for us, matters—a lot! And it's no regular race. It's a race with eternal significance, to win a forever crown. So we should do our very best to live God-honoring lives—to use the gifts God has given us to serve Him and others, to do the good things He has planned for us, and to help others love Jesus and give God all the glory!

Heavenly Father, help me not to forget that every day I'm running an important race You've put me in here on earth. Please help me to run well, looking ahead to a perfect prize in heaven—a crown that will last forever. Amen.

PATIENT PERSEVERANCE

*Be patient, then, brothers and sisters, until the Lord's coming.
See how the farmer waits for the land to yield its valuable crop,
patiently waiting for the autumn and spring rains. You too,
be patient and stand firm, because the Lord's coming is near.
Don't grumble against one another, brothers and sisters, or
you will be judged. The Judge is standing at the door! Brothers
and sisters, as an example of patience in the face of suffering,
take the prophets who spoke in the name of the Lord. As you
know, we count as blessed those who have persevered. You have
heard of Job's perseverance and have seen what the Lord finally
brought about. The Lord is full of compassion and mercy.*

JAMES 5:7–11 NIV

Just as a farmer has to persevere patiently through all sorts
of trials and uncertainties to bring in a valuable crop, we who
follow Jesus also must persevere patiently in life as the Lord
works in this world to bring people to saving faith in Him. Our
attitudes and actions and willingness to be used by God in the
midst of hardship can either help or hinder the spreading of
His truth and love through the gospel.

*Heavenly Father, help me to stand firm and patiently
persevere in all things. I know You are doing good work
gathering people into Your kingdom through Your Son,
Jesus Christ. Please use me in that wonderful work! Amen.*

MAGNIFYING GLASSES

I will praise the name of God with a song,
and will magnify him with thanksgiving.
PSALM 69:30 KJV

When we praise God and offer Him our thanks, we become like transparent glass. All our selfishness and self-centered concerns get out of the way. As the light of God shines through us, we magnify that light. We enable others to see it more easily. We even enable ourselves to see it more easily. The more we praise and thank God, the more clearly we will see His light shining into the darkness of our lives. So go ahead—sing a song of thanksgiving to the Lord. Whether you can carry a tune really doesn't matter!

Thank You, God, for all You have done for
me. I want to magnify Your light.

HUMBLE AND WILLING TO LISTEN

*[Naaman] was a valiant soldier, but he had leprosy. Now
bands of raiders from Aram had gone out and had taken
captive a young girl from Israel, and she served Naaman's
wife. She said to her mistress, "If only my master would see
the prophet who is in Samaria! He would cure him of his
leprosy." Naaman went to his master and told him what
the girl from Israel had said. "By all means, go," the king
of Aram replied. "I will send a letter to the king of Israel."
So Naaman left. . . . The letter that he took to the king
of Israel read: "With this letter I am sending my servant
Naaman to you so that you may cure him of his leprosy."*
2 KINGS 5:1–6 NIV

Naaman was a big deal, yet he must have been a humble man
too—willing to listen to a mere servant girl from Israel who had
been taken captive during a raid and then given to Naaman's
wife. Naaman was soon healed, and he gave God all the glory.
Like Naaman, we too should be humble when we seek answers
and healing from God, never unwilling to listen to even the
meekest among us if they are pointing us to more faith in and
dependence on the one true God of miracles and His perfect
Word.

*Heavenly Father, I want to be a good listener and
follow You well. Guide me through any circumstance
or person, whether impressive or modest. Please
always keep me humble and teachable. Amen.*

POWER OVER EVERY KIND OF EVIL

Once when we were going to the place of prayer, we were met by a female slave who had a spirit by which she predicted the future. She earned a great deal of money for her owners by fortune-telling. She followed Paul and the rest of us, shouting, "These men are servants of the Most High God, who are telling you the way to be saved." She kept this up for many days. Finally Paul became so annoyed that he turned around and said to the spirit, "In the name of Jesus Christ I command you to come out of her!" At that moment the spirit left her.

ACTS 16:16–18 NIV

This poor girl was demon-possessed and a slave to the men making money off of her as she predicted the future. When she met Paul, the demon inside her made her follow Paul and his friends to mock them. But because of the power of Jesus working through Paul, he was able to command the demon to come out of the girl and stop controlling her. Even now, thousands of years later, slavery, demon possession, and mockery of Christians are still happening in our world. But praise God that Jesus has power over every kind of evil and that our hope is in Him to conquer it all!

Dear Jesus, thank You for Your power to rescue people from every evil thing. I pray that You would keep working Your power to rescue people who need it every day. Please show me how I can help! Amen.

SIMPLY HAPPY

Are any of you happy? You should sing praises.
JAMES 5:13 NLT

Some days are simply happy days. The sun shines, people make us laugh, and life seems good. A day like that is a special grace. Thank God for it. As you hum through your day, don't forget to sing His praises.

Father, thank You for the gift of happiness and for life in the Holy Spirit that allows me to sing praises through my days. I praise You with all my heart. Amen.

CONSUMED BY ANGUISH

Be merciful to me, LORD, for I am in distress; my eyes grow weak with sorrow, my soul and body with grief. My life is consumed by anguish and my years by groaning; my strength fails because of my affliction, and my bones grow weak.

PSALM 31:9–10 NIV

Can you relate to the agony in this passage? The book of Psalms includes many instances of wrestling with emotion. These passages are timelessly understandable. Psalms also contains images of great comfort and peace. Notice that after more lament, David, the writer of this psalm, turns to praise and hope again, saying, "But I trust in you, LORD; I say, 'You are my God.' My times are in your hands" (Psalm 31:14–15 NIV).

Dear Lord, like David, the psalmist here, I do feel like my life is consumed by anguish right now. But still I trust in You. I know You are sovereign. You are my one true God. And every moment of my life is in Your hands. Fill me with peace in spite of my pain and show me Your will day by day. Amen.

Day 207

INTERCESSION

We give thanks to God always for you all,
making mention of you in our prayers.
1 Thessalonians 1:2 kjv

There are several different kinds of prayers, from praise to petitions to intercession. Intercession is when we pray on behalf of another person. The Bible makes clear that this type of prayer is a normal and necessary part of following Jesus. We regularly, perhaps even daily, pray for the people in our lives, asking God to bless and help them. There's an aspect of intercession that we don't always consider, though—thanksgiving. Not only do we ask God's blessing on others but we also thank Him for these individuals. We may be surprised to find that, as a result, our relationships with others change and deepen.

Heavenly Friend, I thank You for each of
the people You have put in my life.

PRAISE AND PRAY ALL THE TIME

I will extol the LORD at all times; his praise will always be on my lips. I will glory in the LORD; let the afflicted hear and rejoice. Glorify the LORD with me; let us exalt his name together. I sought the LORD, and he answered me; he delivered me from all my fears. Those who look to him are radiant; their faces are never covered with shame.

PSALM 34:1–5 NIV

It can be hard to be careful with our words. But if praise to God is always on our lips like this psalm says, then there won't be much room for complaints or grumblings or foul language. Another scripture says, "Pray in the Spirit on all occasions with all kinds of prayers and requests" (Ephesians 6:18 NIV). When we do our best to remember these two scriptures, our minds and lips will be busy doing good things that fill us with hope instead of things that fill us with despair and lead us into trouble.

Heavenly Father, I want to be filled with great hope by choosing praise and prayer and keeping them in my mind and on my lips! Amen.

YET THERE IS HOPE

I am sure that our suffering now cannot be compared to the shining-greatness that He is going to give us. Everything that has been made in the world is waiting for the day when God will make His sons known. Everything that has been made in the world is weak. It is not that the world wanted it to be that way. God allowed it to be that way. Yet there is hope. Everything that has been made in the world will be set free from the power that can destroy.
ROMANS 8:18–21 NLV

Often when we're begging God for help and an answer to our prayers, He doesn't just suddenly fix things the way we want. We really wish He would—so when He doesn't, our hope in Him can be shaken as we wonder why. In times like these we must seek wisdom in His Word, from passages like Romans 8, and praise God for the ways He is answering our prayer in other ways, even when we don't see the exact answer we'd like. And we must keep trusting, keep hoping, keep standing strong in faith.

Heavenly Father, please help me to keep trusting You even when I'm feeling confused and discouraged about why You don't answer the way I want You to. Please hold me when I'm hurting and guide me with wisdom from Your Word. Amen.

WONDERFUL PLANS

"For I know the plans I have for you," says the
LORD. *"They are plans for good and not for*
disaster, to give you a future and a hope."
JEREMIAH 29:11 NLT

Don't worry about the future. No matter how frightening it may look to you sometimes, God is waiting there for you. He has plans for you, wonderful plans that will lead you deeper and deeper into His grace and love.

Lord, help me never to waver in the belief that You have good plans for me. When I feel I'm falling headlong into disaster, remind me of my stable future and steady hope. Amen.

VICTORY OVER DEATH

"Death has been swallowed up in victory." "Where, O death, is your victory? Where, O death, is your sting?" The sting of death is sin, and the power of sin is the law. But thanks be to God! He gives us the victory through our Lord Jesus Christ.

1 CORINTHIANS 15:54–57 NIV

God has given us so many reasons to feel grateful. The fact that we no longer have to be afraid of death is just one more reason, but it's a pretty big reason! Through Jesus, death no longer has the last word. The thing that most people fear more than anything no longer has to strike terror into our hearts. In Christ, we will live forever. He has conquered death, and so humanity's age-old enemy no longer has any power over us. Thanks be to God!

Lord Jesus, thank You that on the cross You gave us victory over death. I am so grateful that I no longer need to be afraid of dying. Death will not be an ending but, instead, a doorway into eternity.

WISE CHOICES

*The LORD is the portion of mine inheritance
and of my cup: thou maintainest my lot.*
PSALM 16:5 KJV

Some choices we make change the course of our lives, such as
whether we'll remain single or marry, what career we'll pursue,
whether or not to adopt a child. But there's one choice that
changes not only the direction of our lives but our eternity.
When we choose to follow God, it affects every choice we make
from that moment forward. The more we involve God in our
decision process, the wiser our choices will be.

*God, please fill me with Your life and truth.
Let Your Holy Spirit fill me with wisdom. I take
captive each thought and bring it to You, Jesus.*

HOPE AND HELP FOR HEAVY LOADS

"Come to Me, all of you who work and have heavy loads. I will give you rest. Follow My teachings and learn from Me. I am gentle and do not have pride. You will have rest for your souls. For My way of carrying a load is easy and My load is not heavy."
MATTHEW 11:28–30 NLV

Anytime something feels heavy or troubling in your life, Jesus wants to help you with it. Another scripture says, "Give all your worries to Him because He cares for you" (1 Peter 5:7 NLV). Aren't you glad when you're exhausted and struggling and someone comes along and says, "Let me help you with that"? That's what Jesus is saying here. Talk to Him about every problem you have. Confess your sins to Him. Follow His ways and learn from Him, and you will have the rest and care you need.

Dear Jesus, thank You for letting me come to You with hard and heavy things. Thank You for taking them from me and giving me rest and peace instead. I always want to learn from You and live for You. Amen.

DON'T WORRY; PRAY INSTEAD

Do not be anxious about anything, but in every situation, by prayer and petition, with thanksgiving, present your requests to God. And the peace of God, which transcends all understanding, will guard your hearts and your minds in Christ Jesus.
PHILIPPIANS 4:6–7 NIV

Worry will only make you weak, but prayer packs a powerful punch. When you pray and ask God for what you need, remember to focus on what you've already been given. As you think of the many ways God has already blessed you and provided for you, you'll find yourself wondering, *What is there to worry about? Nothing!* Just like He has in the past, God will continue to bless you and provide for you. Thank Him and praise Him for who He is and all He has done. Then let His amazing peace fill you up so much that there's no room for whatever worries you might have.

Heavenly Father, I don't want to be weak with worry.
Help me to remember the tremendous power in prayer!
Thank You for all the ways You have blessed me and helped me and for all the ways You will continue to do so. Amen.

Day 215

WHAT YOU CRAVE

Take delight in the LORD, and he will
give you your heart's desires.
PSALM 37:4 NLT

Do you ever feel as though God wants to deny you what you want, as though He's a cruel stepparent who takes pleasure in thwarting you? That image of God is a lie. He's the one who placed your heart's desires deep inside you. As you turn to Him, knowing that He alone is the source of all true delight, He will grant you what your heart most truly craves.

Father, I cannot imagine that You love me so much that
You would reach out and give me the things my heart
desires. Yet Your Word is truth. Thank You. Amen.

INDESCRIBABLE

Thanks be to God for his indescribable gift!
2 CORINTHIANS 9:15 NIV

Words are important. How we use them shapes the way we see reality. The more we speak words of gratitude rather than complaints, the more joy we will feel. But sometimes words fail us. God has given us so much, and we can try to describe His many gifts with words. But when it comes right down to it, God's love and blessing are too big for any words to fully express. The Creator of the universe called each one of us into being, and He sustains each of our lives with His love. How can we even wrap our brains around that, let alone put it into words? All we can do is say thank You.

Thank You, God. I don't know what else to say, so I'll just say it again: thank You!

CONFESSION

*Come and listen, all you who fear God, and I will tell
you what he did for me. For I cried out to him for help,
praising him as I spoke. If I had not confessed the sin in my
heart, the Lord would not have listened. But God did listen!
He paid attention to my prayer. Praise God, who did not
ignore my prayer or withdraw his unfailing love from me.*
Psalm 66:16–20 nlt

God always hears our prayers because He is omniscient. He
sees all and knows all. But sometimes He doesn't seem to pay
attention to or answer our prayers. Sometimes that's because
we're holding on to sins in our lives rather than admitting
them to God and asking for His help to get rid of them. James
5:13–16 talks about this subject as well. But there is hope!
Because of Jesus' work on the cross, we can admit all our sins,
ask forgiveness, and be free of them. And when we do, God
pays attention to our prayers.

*Heavenly Father, thank You for Jesus' work on the
cross to free me from my sin. I admit and confess
my sin to You. Thank You for taking it away and
for paying attention to my prayers. Amen.*

ON LEVEL GROUND

Teach me to do your will, for you are my God;
may your good Spirit lead me on level ground.
For your name's sake, LORD, preserve my life;
in your righteousness, bring me out of trouble.
PSALM 143:10–11 NIV

Are you letting God lead you on level ground? How does that show in your life—at home and work and church? In your relationships? In your activities and hobbies? Keep asking God to lead you every day. Let Him guide you out of trouble if you're in it, and let Him steer you away from trouble. Let Him give you the best kind of life because you want to be taught by Him and seek to do His will.

Heavenly Father, I want Your good Spirit inside me to lead me on level ground. Help me to stay out of trouble and follow You no matter what, knowing that You are always right and good. Amen.

GOOD GIFTS

Every good and perfect gift is from above,
coming down from the Father of the heavenly lights,
who does not change like shifting shadows.
JAMES 1:17 NIV

In this verse, James reminds us that each good thing in our life is actually a gift from God. Sometimes we thank God for "spiritual" things, forgetting that we can find God as well in all the lovely details of life—a child's smile, a good meal, a glimpse of a hummingbird, a beautiful sunset, a starry expanse of nighttime sky, a friend's kindness, a pet's loyalty, the light shining through a tree's leaves. All these are reasons to give thanks to God, for they are all gifts of love given to us from His generous hand. We can give Him thanks for more mundane things as well—a good night's sleep, a debt paid off, a smoothly functioning washing machine. Nothing is too little for our gratitude!

Thank You, Father, for Your many gifts.
Thank You that Your generosity never changes.

LESSONS FROM TABITHA

There was a believer in Joppa named Tabitha. . . . She was always doing kind things for others and helping the poor.
ACTS 9:36 NLT

Tabitha was known for being good and kind and making lovely clothing for others. When she became sick and died, two of her friends went to Peter to beg for his help. Her friends knew Peter had been a disciple of Jesus who had the power to heal in His name. Peter agreed and went to the house where they had laid her body. Her friends were gathered around her, crying. Peter told them all to leave the room, and then he knelt down and prayed. Afterward, he said to Tabitha, "Get up," and she opened her eyes and sat up! By the power of Jesus, Peter had healed Tabitha so that she came back to life! Very likely, she then went right back to doing the many good and kind things she loved to do.

Heavenly Father, thank You for the example of Tabitha that inspires me to be generous and to use the talents You've given me to love and encourage others. And thank You for healing her through the power You gave to Peter to show that You are the God of hope and miracles! Amen.

GOD'S HONOR

For the honor of your name, O LORD,
forgive my many, many sins.
PSALM 25:11 NLT

Like all gifts of grace, forgiveness by its very definition is something that can never be earned. Forgiveness is what God gives us when we deserve nothing but anger. He forgives us not because we merit it but because of His own honor. Over and over, we will turn away from God—but over and over, He will bring us back. That is who He is!

Father, I am grateful for Your unending gift of forgiveness. Help me to relish the joy of knowing that You always have and always will continue to forgive my many sins. Amen.

ROAD OF LIFE

*Order my steps in thy word: and let not any
iniquity have dominion over me.*
PSALM 119:133 KJV

When you're driving along an unfamiliar highway, road signs are invaluable. They point you in the proper direction and warn you of impending danger. When it comes to the road of life, the Bible is a sign that helps guide you every step of the way. The more you read it, the better prepared you are to make good choices. When facing a fork in the road of life, stop to consider which direction God's Word would have you go.

*As I hide Your Word in my heart, Lord, please
use it to teach me and guide me. Remind me of
Your truths as I make choices each day.*

STRONGER FAITH

*At once the father cried out. He said with tears in his eyes,
"Lord, I have faith. Help my weak faith to be stronger!"*
MARK 9:24 NLV

If you're struggling to understand what God is doing or not
doing about what you're praying for, remember a story in the
Bible from Mark 9. A father was asking Jesus for help for his
son who was possessed by an evil spirit, but the man struggled
to imagine that Jesus really could do what he was asking. The
father said to Jesus, "Have mercy on us and help us, if you can."
Jesus replied, "What do you mean, 'If I can'? . . . Anything is
possible if a person believes" (Mark 9:22–23 NLT). And the father
said, "Lord, I have faith. Help my weak faith to be stronger!"
When we pray, we must remember that God is able to do exactly
what we ask and so much more! He may or may not answer
the way we ask or expect, but no matter how God responds
to our prayers, our main response to God should be, "Lord, I
have faith. Help my weak faith to be stronger!"

*Heavenly Father, please strengthen my faith and hope in You,
right now and increasingly every day. Thank You! Amen.*

WHEN THE BATTLE IS GOD'S

"Listen, all you people of Judah and Jerusalem! Listen, King Jehoshaphat! This is what the Lord says: Do not be afraid! Don't be discouraged by this mighty army, for the battle is not yours, but God's. . . . You will not even need to fight. Take your positions; then stand still and watch the Lord's victory. He is with you, O people of Judah and Jerusalem. Do not be afraid or discouraged. Go out against them tomorrow, for the Lord is with you!"
2 Chronicles 20:15, 17 nlt

When a problem in your life seems too overwhelming for you to handle, take heart by thinking of this story of King Jehoshaphat in the Bible. God told His people who were up against a great enemy army that the battle was not theirs but His. He told them they wouldn't even need to fight but should just stand and watch His saving power work for them. Sometimes all you need to do is just stand strong in your faith and watch what God does to rescue you from trouble.

Heavenly Father, please show me when I just need to take my position, stand still, and then watch Your victory in the battle going on in my life. I trust You to fight for me! Amen.

TRUE NOURISHMENT

He gives food to every living thing.
His faithful love endures forever.
PSALM 136:25 NLT

People often have a confused relationship with food. We love to eat, but we feel guilty when we do. We sometimes turn to food when we're tense or worried, trying to fill the empty, anxious holes in our hearts. But God wants to give us the true nourishment we need, body and soul, if only we will let Him.

Heavenly Father, any of Your good gifts used for the wrong reasons or in excess have the potential to harm me. Help me to have a healthy relationship with food. Amen.

Day 226

GENEROSITY

*Yes, you will be enriched in every way so that you
can always be generous. And when we take your gifts
to those who need them, they will thank God.*

2 Corinthians 9:11 nlt

We have a special role to play in spreading a spirit of gratitude.
As God gives to us, we have gifts and resources to give to others.
The people we give to are in turn grateful. God's generosity
creates our gratitude, and then our generosity allows others
to be grateful too. It's like a stone dropped in water, its circles
rippling out endlessly, creating continuous cycles of generosity
and gratitude. This is the normal, healthy life of giving and
gratitude to which we are all called by God. God enriches us;
we give to others; we are all united in gratitude.

**Generous God, thank You that You give to
me so that I can give to others.**

JUSTICE

*I will thank the Lord because he is just; I will sing
praise to the name of the Lord Most High.*
Psalm 7:17 nlt

Our world often seems lacking in justice. The poor and the
marginalized always seem to be with us. Our governments
seem less concerned with the needs of ordinary people than
with politics and power. Meanwhile, people become more and
more polarized, unable to agree on even the simplest things.
In the midst of so much confusion, it's good to know that we
serve a just God and, ultimately, His justice will prevail. We
can praise His name with thanksgiving and gratitude, for His
justice, love, and mercy never fail.

*Just God, thank You that when the world seems
full of confusion, You are still in control.*

HOPE FOR WHEN YOU FEEL PERSECUTED

All day long those who hate me have walked on me. For there are many who fight against me with pride. When I am afraid, I will trust in You. I praise the Word of God. I have put my trust in God. I will not be afraid. What can only a man do to me? All day long they change my words to say what I did not say. They are always thinking of ways to hurt me. They go after me as in a fight. . . . Bring down the people in Your anger, O God.
PSALM 56:2–7 NLV

Maybe you can relate to the psalmist here? Maybe you feel like people in your life are hating you and walking all over you and twisting your words and trying to destroy you. But even as all these awful things are happening, the psalmist is putting his hope in God. He's remembering he doesn't need to be afraid of people when the one true, all-powerful God is on His side. And that's what you can remember too.

Heavenly Father, when I feel persecuted, don't let me forget that You see and know what's going on and that You will protect me and fight for me. Amen.

THE LORD WILL WATCH OVER YOU

I will lift up my eyes to the mountains. Where will my help come from? My help comes from the Lord, Who made heaven and earth. He will not let your feet go out from under you. He Who watches over you will not sleep. Listen, He Who watches over Israel will not close his eyes or sleep. The Lord watches over you. The Lord is your safe cover at your right hand. The sun will not hurt you during the day and the moon will not hurt you during the night. The Lord will keep you from all that is sinful. He will watch over your soul. The Lord will watch over your coming and going, now and forever.

PSALM 121 NLV

No one cares for you or watches over you as well as God does. He does not get tired; He never needs to sleep. Every time you need a fresh dose of hope and help, look up to remember that He is Creator of the mountains and the heavens and the earth— and don't forget that He is within you through His Spirit too.

Heavenly Father, You are my constant hope and helper and hero. Thank You for always watching over me, now and forever. Amen.

SPECIAL PEOPLE

I thank my God every time I remember you.
PHILIPPIANS 1:3 NIV

God has put certain people in our lives who are particular blessings to us. Whether they are friends or family, they are the individuals who have made a difference in who we are. Their love and support have shaped us and helped us to see both God and ourselves more clearly. When we think of these people, our hearts leap with thanksgiving, for these individuals are very special gifts to us from God. He has used them as vehicles for His love. Because of them, we are blessed. With each cherished memory that crosses our minds, we are touched by love and thanksgiving.

God, thank You for the special people in my life. May my heart leap up in gratitude to You each time they cross my mind.

PERSPECTIVE AND SOLACE

*The LORD also will be a refuge for the oppressed,
a refuge in times of trouble. And they that know
thy name will put their trust in thee: for thou,
LORD, hast not forsaken them that seek thee.*
PSALM 9:9–10 KJV

When women are in need of comfort, they seem to instinctively turn to a spouse or close friend. There's nothing wrong with seeking a human shoulder to cry on when you need it. Just remember that the Bible refers to Jesus as both our bridegroom and our friend. The comfort God provides runs deeper than anything people can offer. God sees your problems as part of a larger, eternal picture and can offer perspective as well as solace.

*Jesus, You are my friend and perfect
counselor. Change my desires so that I run
to You first before I go to others. Help me to
understand the reality of who You are.*

DARKNESS INTO LIGHT

And I will lead the blind in a way that they do not know, in paths that they have not known I will guide them. I will turn the darkness before them into light, the rough places into level ground. These are the things I do, and I do not forsake them.

ISAIAH 42:16 ESV

When we're facing big problems or have big choices to make, sometimes we feel totally blind, like we just can't see the right way to go or the best thing to do. So the promises and hope God gives in this scripture are soothing and refreshing. We can trust that He will turn the darkness into light and make the rough places smooth for His people. He will open up new paths for us when we don't know what to do or where to go. He never leaves us to face anything alone, and He never breaks a promise.

Heavenly Father, I'm hoping and trusting in You because I know You keep Your promises. And You have promised to guide Your people well. Please guide me right now. Show me Your will and Your way for my life. Amen.

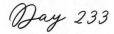
Day 233

HEARTFELT

For we live by believing and not by seeing.
2 CORINTHIANS 5:7 NLT

The world of science tells us that only what can be seen and measured is truly real. But our hearts know differently. Every day, we depend on the things we believe—our faith in God and in our friends and family, our commitment to give ourselves to God and others—and it is these invisible beliefs that give us grace to live.

Father, my mind is so prone to cling to what is tangible. However, my heart is sure that You are as real as the bright shining sun. Fill me with confidence and trust. Amen.

NO MATTER THE PAST

*Jesus said to her, "Mary." She turned and said to him in
Aramaic, "Rabboni!" (which means Teacher). Jesus said to her,
"Do not cling to me, for I have not yet ascended to the Father;
but go to my brothers and say to them, 'I am ascending to
my Father and your Father, to my God and your God.'" Mary
Magdalene went and announced to the disciples, "I have
seen the Lord"—and that he had said these things to her.*
JOHN 20:16–18 ESV

Mary Magdalene had a terrible life before she met Jesus. He
cast seven demons out of her (Luke 8:2), and she was beyond
grateful and became a close follower. When Jesus was crucified,
Mary Magdalene was there and must have been devastated.
But then she was also there when Jesus rose from the dead,
and we can only imagine the joy she must have felt! She was
the very first to see Jesus again after He had come back to life.
Mary Magdalene's story offers tremendous hope to anyone
who has experienced a terrible life before coming to trust in
Jesus. He has the power to completely transform, renew, and
bless anyone's life—no matter their past.

*Heavenly Father, help me to remember that no one is hopeless.
You have all power to rescue anyone from any terrible situation
and then transform and renew and bless them incredibly. Amen.*

SLEEP SOUNDLY

*You can go to bed without fear; you will lie down
and sleep soundly. You need not be afraid of sudden
disaster or the destruction that comes upon the
wicked, for the LORD is your security.*
PROVERBS 3:24–26 NLT

Whether we let ourselves get enough or not, we all know how important sleep is. And no one can heal from any illness, injury, or pain—whether physical or emotional or both—unless they take time to let the body and mind rest. When you hope and trust in God, seeking Him and consistently following the wisdom of His Word, He will give you the rest and peace you need.

Heavenly Father, help me to remember how important rest is. Help me to be still and know that You are God! I hope in You and follow You. Please give me sweet, sound, healing slumber and Your peace that passes all understanding. Amen.

REACH OUT TO HIM

*"Your words have supported those who were falling;
you encouraged those with shaky knees."*

JOB 4:4 NLT

God knows how weak and shaky we feel some days. He understands our feelings. After all, He made us, so He understands how prone humans are to discouragement. He doesn't blame us for being human, but He never leaves us helpless either. His grace is always there, like a hand held out to us, simply waiting for us to reach out and grasp it.

Lord, thank You for Your words that give me support and hope when I am falling. Thank You for encouraging me when I feel shaky. May I rest in Your grace and truth. Amen.

CONFUSED

They knew God, but they wouldn't worship him as God or even give him thanks. And they began to think up foolish ideas of what God was like. As a result, their minds became dark and confused.

ROMANS 1:21 NLT

Again and again, the Bible makes clear to us how important gratitude is to our spiritual and emotional well-being. It's not enough to go to church. It's not enough to talk about God or memorize the Bible. We need to have an intimate relationship with Him, one that is based on love and thanksgiving. Without that, everything else is empty—and we are bound to get confused, our thoughts dark and bewildered. But as we worship God, as we lift up our hearts in gratitude for all He has done for us, slowly the light streams back into our lives again. Things become clear once more.

Dear Lord, I want my relationship with You to be real and close. I thank You so much for everything You have done for me.

YOU ARE WEAK; GOD IS NOT

*Christ is not weak when He works in your hearts.
He uses His power in you. Christ's weak human body
died on a cross. It is by God's power that Christ lives
today. We are weak. We are as He was. But we will be
alive with Christ through the power God has for us.*
2 CORINTHIANS 13:3–4 NLV

When you're feeling weak, don't feel hopeless, and don't beat yourself up. The truth is that you *are* weak as a human being in your human body. But God is not weak. Remember that, with the Holy Spirit in you, you have the same power that raised Jesus from death to life working in you. That's incredible! Whatever God has planned for you to do, you can trust that you will be able to do it well. He will give you the gifts and strengths and tools you need to do it. And someday, God's power in you will enable you to live forever in heaven too!

Heavenly Father, thank You that You are never weak. You are my strength. You are my power. You are my hope. Amen.

MENDING A BROKEN HEART

The Lord is nigh unto them that are of a broken heart; and saveth such as be of a contrite spirit.
PSALM 34:18 KJV

Putting your faith in Jesus doesn't mean you'll never have a broken heart. Scripture tells us that even Jesus wept. Jesus knew the future. He knew His heavenly Father was in control. He knew victory was certain. But He still grieved. When your heart is broken, only God has the power to make it whole again. It won't happen overnight. But when you draw close to God, you draw close to the true source of peace, joy, and healing.

You are so close to me when I'm hurting, Father. Thank You that I don't have to go through this alone. I offer up all my feelings to You. Please bring comfort and peace.

SHINE A LIGHT OF HOPE
IN THE WORLD

*Do all things without grumbling or disputing, that you
may be blameless and innocent, children of God without
blemish in the midst of a crooked and twisted generation,
among whom you shine as lights in the world.*

PHILIPPIANS 2:14–15 ESV

It's extremely difficult to do *all* things without grumbling or
complaining. Yet that's what we should strive for. A good
attitude is something we all need enormous help from
God to cultivate. But if we can stay positive as we obey God
and follow the plans He has for us, we shine as extra-bright
lights to the sinful world around us. And, just maybe, people
who don't yet trust in Jesus as their Savior will want to know
more about God's love and peace in us because they see His
light shining in our attitudes and actions.

*Heavenly Father, please help me to shine Your
light of hope in the darkness of sin around me in
this world. I want to shine brightly so others might
come to know Jesus as Savior too. Amen.*

Day 241

CLEANSED

Don't you realize that those who do wrong will not inherit the Kingdom of God? Don't fool yourselves. Those who indulge in sexual sin, or who worship idols, or commit adultery, or are male prostitutes, or practice homosexuality, or are thieves, or greedy people, or drunkards, or are abusive, or cheat people—none of these will inherit the Kingdom of God. Some of you were once like that. But you were cleansed; you were made holy; you were made right with God by calling on the name of the Lord Jesus Christ and by the Spirit of our God.
1 CORINTHIANS 6:9–11 NLT

So much hope and healing can be found in the amazing grace Jesus offers to anyone who believes in Him. Any sin can be cleansed by the blood of Jesus' sacrifice of Himself on the cross for the sins of all people. "'Come now, let's settle this,' says the LORD. 'Though your sins are like scarlet, I will make them as white as snow. Though they are red like crimson, I will make them as white as wool'" (Isaiah 1:18 NLT).

Dear Jesus, thank You that anyone can call on You to be cleansed and saved from sin because You sacrificed Yourself on the cross to pay the penalty. Please keep calling me and all people everywhere to sincere repentance and steadfast hope in You.

LEADING

But since we belong to the day, let us be sober, putting on faith and love as a breastplate, and the hope of salvation as a helmet.
1 THESSALONIANS 5:8 NIV

We sometimes think of discipline as a negative thing, as something that asks us to sacrifice and punish ourselves. But really the word has more to do with the grace we receive from instruction and learning, from following a master. Like an athlete who follows her coach's leading, we are called to follow our Master, wearing His uniform of love and His helmet of hope.

Heavenly Father, You are my master, my guide, my coach, my everything. Thank You for Your grace and for giving me the tools I need to be self-controlled, faithful, loving, and hopeful. Amen.

THANKFUL SURRENDER

Make thankfulness your sacrifice to God.
PSALM 50:14 NLT

When we think about God asking us to make a sacrifice, we imagine that He wants us to give up something we enjoy. We are like Abraham, who believed God wanted him to kill his son on an altar when what God really wanted wasn't for Abraham to take his son's life but, instead, for Abraham to offer him totally to God with joy and thanksgiving. There may be times when God *will* ask us to give up a particular behavior or habit, but only because He knows it's not good for us, not because He likes to take things away from us. Instead, He asks us to dedicate every part of our lives to Him, to stop claiming them for ourselves, and to make thankfulness our daily sacrifice.

Thank You, God, for all You have given me. May my daily thanksgiving be an act of surrender to Your love.

NONE LIKE THE ONE TRUE GOD

No pagan god is like you, O Lord. None can do what you do! All the nations you made will come and bow before you, Lord; they will praise your holy name. For you are great and perform wonderful deeds. You alone are God.
PSALM 86:8–10 NLT

When your hope is in the one true God, it is in exactly the right place—because nothing and no one else is like Him. The false gods and religions and spiritual ways of this world offer only empty, untrue hope. Only the one true God offers real grace and salvation through the gift of His Son, Jesus Christ, whom He sent as a sacrifice to pay for the sin of everyone who trusts in Him. Jesus alone covers our sin and offers eternal life and relationship with God, not because of anything we do, but simply when we surrender, repent of sin, and believe in Him to save us. He said, "I am the way, the truth, and the life. No one can come to the Father except through me" (John 14:6 NLT).

Magnificent God, You alone are the one true God, and I bow before You and praise You! I thank You for saving me and giving me every reason to hope because Your Son, Jesus Christ, has paid for my sin. I trust in You alone. Amen.

HEALING FROM PAST SIN

The Lord is merciful and gracious, slow to anger and abounding in steadfast love. He will not always chide, nor will he keep his anger forever. He does not deal with us according to our sins, nor repay us according to our iniquities. For as high as the heavens are above the earth, so great is his steadfast love toward those who fear him; as far as the east is from the west, so far does he remove our transgressions from us.

Psalm 103:8–12 esv

Our enemy Satan doesn't want us to heal from our past sins. He wants us to agonize over them endlessly, beat ourselves up, and live in dejection and defeat so that we feel far away from God. But the truth is that when we repent of our sins, God takes them as far away from us as possible—"as far as the east is from the west"—so that we can draw as close to Him as possible. He is merciful and gracious and loving. He wants to completely heal our hearts and minds from the sins of our past so that we live in spiritual and mental wellness and victory, ready and able to do every good thing He has planned for us.

Heavenly Father, please help me never to agonize over past sin I have repented of. I know You have completely removed it from me. I can't ever thank You enough. Your mercy, grace, and love are far greater than I deserve, and I am grateful! Amen.

Day 246

LAW OF LOVE

I pondered the direction of my life,
and I turned to follow your laws.
PSALM 119:59 NLT

Did you know that the word *law* comes from root words that mean "foundation" or "something firm and fixed"? Sometimes we can't help but feel confused and uncertain. When that happens, turn to God's law, His rule for living. Love is His law, the foundation that always holds firm. When we cling to that, we find direction.

Lord, when I ponder the direction of my life without Your Spirit, I am lost and uncertain. Thank You for Your Word that anchors me in truth and provides the guidance I need. Amen.

OUR SOUL

To the end that my glory may sing praise to thee, and not be silent. O LORD my God, I will give thanks unto thee for ever.
PSALM 30:12 KJV

The word that the King James Version of the Bible translates as "glory" also means "soul." It is the part of each of us that makes us who we are; it is the unique light that God placed within us, the thing that makes us shine in our individual ways. This innermost part of our being—our soul—is the place where God calls us to sing out His praises. It is here where gratitude lives within us, making our inner glory gleam with grace as we offer back to God all that He has so generously given to us.

God of grace, may I shine with Your love as I give You thanks for all You do for me.

HOPE FOR HAVING A CHILD

*Zechariah and Elizabeth were righteous in God's eyes,
careful to obey all of the Lord's commandments and
regulations. They had no children because Elizabeth
was unable to conceive, and they were both very old.*

LUKE 1:6–7 NLT

Elizabeth and her husband, Zechariah, both thought they were
far too old to have children, but God sent the angel Gabriel to
tell Zechariah that Elizabeth would have a son and they should
name him John. Zechariah didn't believe it, and because of his
unbelief God made him unable to speak. But soon Elizabeth
became pregnant. "'How kind the Lord is!' she exclaimed.
'He has taken away my disgrace of having no children'" (Luke
1:25 NLT).

*Heavenly Father, remind me through the story of Elizabeth
and Zechariah and their miracle son, John, that even
when things seem totally impossible, there is always
hope because You work in miraculous ways according
to Your perfect will and perfect plans. Amen.*

GOD'S COMMITMENT

*He hath remembered his covenant for ever, the word
which he commanded to a thousand generations.*
Psalm 105:8 kjv

God has made a commitment to you similar to a wedding vow.
He promises to love and cherish you through sickness and
health, prosperity or poverty, good times and bad. But with
God, this commitment doesn't last until "death do you part."
Even in death and beyond, God is there. There's nothing you
can do that will make Him turn His face from you. His commitment to love and forgive you stands steadfast, come what may.

*Your Word tells me that nothing—absolutely nothing, not
even death—can separate me from Your love, Lord. I rest in
that truth. My confidence and stability is in You alone.*

FOCUS ON THE POSITIVE

I will give thanks to you, LORD, with all my heart;
I will tell of all your wonderful deeds.
PSALM 9:1 NIV

One way to build gratitude in our lives and in the lives of others is to focus our speech on the good things God has done for us. Too often when we're talking with our friends, we tend to complain rather than give thanks. We describe the negative things in our lives in great detail while overlooking the positive things, both big and small. The more we feel gratitude in our hearts, the more it will spill out into our conversation. And the reverse is true as well: the more we speak of our gratitude for all life's gifts, the more we will experience thanksgiving in our hearts.

May my speech be full of thanksgiving,
Lord, rather than complaints.

IMAGINE THE BEST, NOT THE WORST

God is our safe place and our strength. He is always our help when we are in trouble. So we will not be afraid, even if the earth is shaken and the mountains fall into the center of the sea, and even if its waters go wild with storm and the mountains shake with its action.
PSALM 46:1–3 NLV

Sometimes we feel hopeless and full of fear because we imagine the worst that can happen and then focus on that. So we need this scripture to remind us that there is no horrible thing we can think of that God cannot deliver us from. He is always our help when we are in trouble, no matter how awful the situation. Instead of imagining the worst, we should focus on the best—the truth that God is our safe place and our strength!

Heavenly Father, I trust that You will protect and save me from even the worst kind of trouble. Thank You that You will always be my hope and my help. Amen.

SHARE YOUR GIFTS

God has given each of you a gift from his great variety of
spiritual gifts. Use them well to serve one another. Do you have
the gift of speaking? Then speak as though God himself were
speaking through you. Do you have the gift of helping others?
Do it with all the strength and energy that God supplies.
Then everything you do will bring glory to God through
Jesus Christ. All glory and power to him forever and ever!
1 PETER 4:10–11 NLT

God has given you special gifts, but they are not for you alone.
Don't ever just keep them to yourself. Share your gifts with
others—those talents and abilities and skills that come easily to
you. God has given them to you so you can serve and encourage
and bless others. If you don't already know, pray and ask God
to help you recognize the things you're especially good at and
exactly how He wants you to use those abilities. Most of all,
constantly thank God and give credit to Him for every wonderful thing you can do. Every good thing is a gift from Him.

Heavenly Father, thank You for the talents and abilities
You have given me. Help me to know how best to use
them to share Your hope and love. I want to worship
You and bless and encourage others. Amen.

NEW INSIGHT

Your word is a lamp to guide my feet and a light for my path.
PSALM 119:105 NLT

We sometimes take the scriptures for granted. These ancient words, though, continue to shine with light just as they did centuries ago. In them, God's grace is revealed to us. In them, we gain new insight into ourselves and our lives.

Father, every time I open Your Word, I am blessed by a fresh revelation of Your truth. May Your ancient words drip like sweet honey into the depths of my soul. Amen.

DON'T FOCUS ON FEARS

I will honor the Lord at all times. His praise will always be in my mouth. My soul will be proud to tell about the Lord. Let those who suffer hear it and be filled with joy. Give great honor to the Lord with me. Let us praise His name together. I looked for the Lord, and He answered me. And He took away all my fears. They looked to Him and their faces shined with joy.

PSALM 34:1–5 NLV

What are you fearing right now? How are you battling those fears and choosing not to focus on them? They grow bigger in your mind if you let them have a lot of room in there. So don't! Instead, give God a lot of room in your mind. Focus on Him rather than fear by reading His Word, singing praises to Him, and praying to Him. Ask Him to show Himself to you in all kinds of ways. Then wait and see how He takes away all your fears and replaces them with hope and peace and joy!

Heavenly Father, please help me to take my focus off my fears and put it on You instead. Fill my mind and heart with hope and peace and joy because my thoughts are on You and full of praise to You! Amen.

HE COMMANDS EVEN WINDS AND WATER

One day he got into a boat with his disciples, and he said to them, "Let us go across to the other side of the lake." So they set out, and as they sailed he fell asleep. And a windstorm came down on the lake, and they were filling with water and were in danger. And they went and woke him, saying, "Master, Master, we are perishing!" And he awoke and rebuked the wind and the raging waves, and they ceased, and there was a calm. He said to them, "Where is your faith?" And they were afraid, and they marveled, saying to one another, "Who then is this, that he commands even winds and water, and they obey him?"

LUKE 8:22–25 ESV

Jesus can command anything in all creation to obey Him. He could simply speak words to a storm to make it stop. He has extraordinary, supernatural power over everything, and He's your Savior who loves and cares for you. Remembering these truths can fill you with great hope and courage to face any hard thing.

Dear Jesus, You can speak the words to stop the storm in my life. But even if You don't right now, You will eventually in Your perfect timing. Most importantly, I know You won't leave me in the midst of the storm. I put my trust and hope in You alone. Amen.

CONSISTENTLY COMMITTED

*But I will hope continually, and will yet
praise thee more and more.*
PSALM 71:14 KJV

Choosing to follow God is not a one-time commitment. It's a choice that's made anew each day. Who, or what, will you choose to follow today? Culture and popular opinion? Your emotions and desires? Or God and His Word? Staying consistently committed to anything—a diet, an exercise program, a spouse, or God—takes effort. But with God, His own Spirit strengthens us and gives us hope to help us remain fully committed to Him.

*God, please let Your Spirit rise up in me to teach
me and lead me. Show me how to listen for Your
voice in my life. Teach me to do Your will.*

EVER WIDER

A longing fulfilled is a tree of life.
PROVERBS 13:12 NIV

Take stock of your life. What were you most hoping to achieve a year ago? (Or five years ago?) How many of those goals have been achieved? Sometimes, once we've reached a goal, we move on too quickly to the next one and never allow ourselves to find the grace God wants to reveal within that achievement. With each goal reached, His grace spreads out into your life like a tree whose branches grow ever wider.

God, help me to find the balance between moving forward and looking back. Give me moments to pause and reflect on how far I have come with Your grace. Amen.

GOOD MEDICINE

*A cheerful heart is good medicine, but a
broken spirit saps a person's strength.*
PROVERBS 17:22 NLT

Everyone has heard that "laughter is the best medicine." And it's
so true that doing our best to have a cheerful attitude and a good
sense of humor, even in the midst of struggle or pain or grief,
has a huge impact on how quickly and well we heal from any
kind of illness or injury. Depression, or a broken spirit, totally
saps a person's strength—this scripture tells us so, and we've
all either witnessed it in others or experienced it ourselves.
So keep laughing. Keep looking for things to smile about and
be grateful for. Ask God to show you when you can't see any
yourself. And remember that "for the despondent, every day
brings trouble; for the happy heart, life is a continual feast"
(Proverbs 15:15 NLT).

*Heavenly Father, even in the worst of times, please give me
a supernaturally happy heart and a good sense of humor.
Help me to focus on blessings. Use laughter and joy and
gratitude to help heal and restore me, please. Amen.*

NO GREATER HOPE

*For God so loved the world that he gave his one
and only Son, that whoever believes in him
shall not perish but have eternal life.*

JOHN 3:16 NIV

John 3:16 is one of the most famous and popular verses in all of the Bible. Because it is so well known, sometimes we overlook it or forget its significance. But we really need to stop and dwell on it at times, for it succinctly tells of God's extraordinary love. He loves you and everyone in the world *so* much that He gave up His only Son, Jesus, to die on the cross to pay the price for the sin of every person. And then Jesus rose to life again, showing how He conquers death and gives forever life to those who humble themselves, repent of sin, and believe in Him as Savior. There is no greater hope!

Heavenly Father, thank You for the love and hope You have given me and all people because You sent Jesus to die to save the world from the punishment of sin. Thank You that He rose to life again and that I have forever life too because I believe in Him as my one and only Savior. Help me to share the good news of Your great love! Amen.

WISE ENOUGH TO LEAD

*"To God belong wisdom and power;
counsel and understanding are his."*
JOB 12:13 NIV

The word *wisdom* comes from the same root words that have to do with vision, the ability to see into a deeper spiritual reality. Where else can we turn for the grace to see beneath life's surface except to God? Who else can we trust to be strong enough and wise enough to lead us to our eternal home?

Lord, my vision is far from twenty-twenty. Help me see the world through Your lens of wisdom. Bestow on me Your counsel, and fill me with Your understanding. Amen.

OUTSIDE OF TIME'S STREAM

Your throne, O Lord, has stood from time immemorial.
You yourself are from the everlasting past.
PSALM 93:2 NLT

If you think of time as a fast-moving river, then we are creatures caught in its stream. Life keeps slipping away from us like water between our fingers. But God is outside of time's stream. He holds our past safely in His hands, and His grace is permanent and unshakable. His love is the lifesaver to which we cling in the midst of time's wild waves.

God, when I try to understand words like immemorial *and* everlasting, *I am in awe. I cannot begin to comprehend Your bigness. Give me Your perspective. Help me to trust You. Amen.*

COMPASSION

*Like as a father pitieth his children,
so the LORD pitieth them that fear him.*
PSALM 103:13 KJV

If your children are hurting, you don't think twice about coming to their aid. You listen attentively to their heartaches, dry their tears, and offer them words of wisdom and encouragement. As God's child, you have a perfect and powerful heavenly Father who feels this way about you. His compassion is more than emotion. It's love in action. You can tell God anything without fear of condemnation or abandonment. God's forgiveness runs as deep as His love.

God, please restore my heart's ability to see You as a loving Father. I repent of any thoughts that paint You as anything but loving and perfect. Because of Jesus, I stand before You, holy and pleasing in Your sight.

KEPT IN THE LOVE OF GOD

*But you, beloved, building yourselves up in your
most holy faith and praying in the Holy Spirit, keep
yourselves in the love of God, waiting for the mercy
of our Lord Jesus Christ that leads to eternal life.*

JUDE 1:20–21 ESV

How do you keep yourself in the love of God? Do you spend time learning from Him? Do you regularly read His Word? Do you talk to God through prayer and have quiet time to listen for answers? Do you go to a Bible-teaching church to worship and learn? Do you serve Jesus by serving others? Do you have other strong Christians in your life who help remind you of and encourage you in God's truth and love? Do you fill your mind with songs of praise to Him? Through His Holy Spirit, God is with you always, but sometimes it's easy to ignore His presence. We have to be diligent and intentional to keep ourselves in His love.

*Heavenly Father, I want to keep myself in Your
love, staying in close relationship with You!
Please help me to never forget or ignore You. Amen.*

FORGET NOT ALL HIS BENEFITS

Praise the LORD, my soul; all my inmost being, praise his holy name. Praise the LORD, my soul, and forget not all his benefits—who forgives all your sins and heals all your diseases, who redeems your life from the pit and crowns you with love and compassion, who satisfies your desires with good things so that your youth is renewed like the eagle's.
PSALM 103:1–5 NIV

If you're struggling with hopelessness or discouragement today, have you forgotten all God's benefits to you? Don't look around to see what others have been blessed with that you have not. Look inwardly and at the life God has given specifically to you and thank Him for every blessing, for even every single breath you take. You have life because He has given it to you. And you have purpose and joy when you live your life *in* Christ and *for* Christ, focusing on Him above all else and praising Him for every good thing He gives along your journey.

Heavenly Father, please forgive me when I forget all Your benefits to me. Help me not to compare my life and blessings with the lives and blessings of others. Instead, help me to live the unique life You have given me with gratitude and for Your glory. Amen.

VEHICLE FOR GOD'S GRACE

*Do not neglect your gift. . . . Be diligent in
these matters; give yourself wholly to them,
so that everyone may see your progress.*
1 TIMOTHY 4:14–15 NIV

God expects us to use the talents He gave us. Don't turn away
from them with a false sense of modesty. Exercise them.
Improve your skills. Whatever your gift may be, use it as a
vehicle for God's grace.

*Lord, help me not to bury my talents. Give me courage and
boldness to use the gifts You have given me, knowing the
more I use them, the stronger my gifts will be. Amen.*

CARRIERS OF GOD'S GRACE

*I always thank my God for you because of
his grace given you in Christ Jesus.*
1 CORINTHIANS 1:4 NIV

Think of the people in your life who bring you joy. Their smiles, their hugs, their understanding, and their unconditional love help to make life worth living. Now consider: Each one of those individuals is a gift from God. Each one carries His grace to you in a unique way. Each one bears Christ Jesus into your life. It's easy to take others for granted—but when we think about the individuals around us in this light, our hearts will overflow with thanksgiving. God brings these special people into our lives to show us how much He loves us.

*Thank You, Jesus, for showing me Your face
through the people who love me.*

TELL THE WORLD

Give thanks to the LORD and proclaim his greatness.
Let the whole world know what he has done.
1 CHRONICLES 16:8 NLT

When we're truly excited about something, we can hardly keep silent about it. Thankfulness is a personal feeling, an intimate emotion that we cherish deep in our hearts. It can be a quiet sense of gratitude that we privately return to again and again throughout our days. At the same time, though, thankfulness spills over. It tells the world what God has done. That doesn't mean we need to become obnoxious people who shove our beliefs about God down others' throats. In quiet and sometimes understated ways, though, our gratitude will shine out from us. Through our lives, the whole world will see God's amazing love in action.

God, may my life be an unending story of gratitude to You.

PROVEN FAITH

Shadrach, Meshach and Abednego replied to him,
"King Nebuchadnezzar, we do not need to defend ourselves
before you in this matter. If we are thrown into the blazing
furnace, the God we serve is able to deliver us from it,
and he will deliver us from Your Majesty's hand."
DANIEL 3:16–17 NIV

We prove that our faith in God is real when we keep on trusting in God even if things don't go the way we hoped and prayed for and were confident of at first. Shadrach, Meshach, and Abednego were true heroes of the faith. They believed without a doubt that God could save them from the blazing furnace, but they went on to tell King Nebuchadnezzar, "Even if he does not, we want you to know, Your Majesty, that we will not serve your gods or worship the image of gold you have set up" (Daniel 3:18 NIV).

Heavenly Father, I want to prove that my faith in
You is 100 percent real. I will never worship anyone
but You, even if You don't answer my prayers the
way I know You can and hope You will. Amen.

HOPE FOR FORGIVENESS

"If you forgive those who sin against you, your heavenly Father will forgive you. But if you refuse to forgive others, your Father will not forgive your sins."
MATTHEW 6:14–15 NLT

There is no hope for forgiveness for us if we don't forgive others. It's not always easy to do, but the Bible is clear that it's a big deal. Jesus said that God won't forgive our sins if we don't forgive others. And we know how much we need Him to forgive our sins and mistakes! Because we are forgiven so generously through Jesus' work on the cross, we should want to forgive generously as well.

Dear Jesus, when I struggle to forgive, help me to think about how thankful I am that You forgive my sin. I want to follow Your example. Amen.

GOD OF OUR ANCESTORS

"I thank and praise you, God of my ancestors:
You have given me wisdom and power."
DANIEL 2:23 NIV

Genealogists tell us that over twelve generations and four hundred years, it took 4,094 ancestors to lead to the birth of each one of us. Think of all those individuals who suffered and rejoiced, toiled and sacrificed, lived and died! If just one of them had died without bearing children, we would not be here today. But God was with our ancestors back through the generations. He was already blessing us four hundred years ago. . .and four thousand years ago. He did not forsake our ancestors—and He will not forsake us. We have so many reasons to give Him thanks!

God of my ancestors, I thank You for Your faithfulness
down through the generations. May I make good use of the
foundation You have given me and grow in wisdom and power.

Day 271

WHERE CREDIT IS DUE

*It is not that we think we are qualified to do anything
on our own. Our qualification comes from God.*
2 Corinthians 3:5 nlt

It's easy to seek God when we feel like failures, but when success comes our way, we like to congratulate ourselves rather than give God the credit. When we achieve great things, we need to remember that it is God's grace through us that brought about our success.

*Father, every good thing I do comes from You.
Thank You for allowing me to collaborate with You to do
Your work. It is an honor to be used by You. Amen.*

THE HEAVENLY FATHER'S EMBRACE

But thou, O Lord, art a God full of compassion, and gracious,
long suffering, and plenteous in mercy and truth.
PSALM 86:15 KJV

Without love and compassion, an all-powerful God would be
something to fear instead of someone to trust. That's one reason
why Jesus came to earth: to help us see the compassionate
side of the Almighty. Throughout the gospels, we read how
Jesus reached out to the hurting—the outcasts, the infirm, the
poor, and the abandoned. He didn't turn his back on sinners
but embraced them with open arms. His arms are still open.
Will you run toward His embrace?

Thank You, God, for sending Jesus to make a way
for me to approach You in full confidence. You have
lifted up my head and showered me with love and
compassion. Help me to feel Your presence in my life.

IT'S A TRAP

Yet true godliness with contentment is itself great wealth. After all, we brought nothing with us when we came into the world, and we can't take anything with us when we leave it. So if we have enough food and clothing, let us be content. But people who long to be rich fall into temptation and are trapped by many foolish and harmful desires that plunge them into ruin and destruction. For the love of money is the root of all kinds of evil. And some people, craving money, have wandered from the true faith and pierced themselves with many sorrows.
1 TIMOTHY 6:6–10 NLT

The Bible is clear that it's total foolishness to put our hope in money and wealth. It's a trap. And those who get caught in this trap often venture into all kinds of sin and harmful things that result in their total destruction. We must ask God to help us put all our hope in Him rather than in wealth and worldly success. He will give us goals that match up with His good plans for our lives, according to the gifts and talents He has given us.

Heavenly Father, please help me never to make my hopes and goals about money; I want them to be about serving You and giving You glory! Please help me keep my focus on all the best things You have planned for me. Amen.

GOD IS ALWAYS STRONGER

The One Who lives in you is stronger than the one who is in the world.

1 JOHN 4:4 NLV

The world can feel absolutely upside down these days. How are you noticing that lately? We have an enemy, the devil, who loves to spread sin and evil as much as he can (1 Peter 5:8, 1 John 5:19). Yet even when things seem out of control in the world around you, you always have hope and power and strength because of God's Holy Spirit living in you. Memorize 1 John 4:4 and then put it on repeat in your mind. God is *always* stronger than the devil. God never leaves you and will help you fight and win against any evil plan the enemy has against you.

Heavenly Father, don't let me forget that You are always stronger within me than the evil one who is in the world. Give me strength and courage and hope and confidence as I remember the power of Your Word and Your Holy Spirit within me. Amen.

Day 275

WELCOME INTERRUPTIONS

So they left by boat for a quiet place, where they could be alone.
MARK 6:32 NLT

Jesus and the disciples sought a quiet place, away from the crowds. Like us, they needed alone time. But as so often happens, people interrupt those moments of solitude. The crowd follows us, the phone rings, someone comes to the door. When that happens, we must ask Jesus for the grace to follow His example and let go of our quiet moments alone, welcoming the interruption with patience and love.

Jesus, I am good at setting my own agenda. Help me to see life's interruptions as gifts from You, rather than disruptions to my "perfect" plan. Amen.

OTHERS' LIVES

*Dear brothers and sisters, we can't help but thank
God for you, because your faith is flourishing
and your love for one another is growing.*
2 THESSALONIANS 1:3 NLT

God has given us many reasons to be thankful. Each of our lives overflows with blessings, even in the midst of troubles and suffering. But have you ever considered thanking God for all that He is doing in others' lives? Look at the lives of your children, your husband, your extended family, and your friends. Pay attention to what God is doing in and through them. As you notice their faith flourish and their love grow, you can affirm God's working within their lives, giving them encouragement and new strength—and you'll also have one more reason to offer up gratitude to God.

Thank You, dear Lord, for all You are doing in my loved ones' lives. I see Your hand at work, and I praise You.

ETERNALLY CONFIDENT

*My heart is fixed, O God, my heart is
fixed: I will sing and give praise.*
Psalm 57:7 kjv

In the Bible, when a word or phrase is repeated, it's time to pay
attention. In the original language of the Old Testament, this
signifies that something is the best, the ultimate, the pièce de
résistance! The psalmist in Psalm 57 doubly notes how confident
his heart is in God. No wonder praise comes naturally to him!
Take it from the psalmist: You need never doubt God's heart
toward you. You can be confident—eternally confident—in Him.

*Just like the psalmist, I want my heart to be fixed on You, Lord.
Please give me the desire to know You more! Help me to want
the things You want and to see things the way You see them.*

THE PRIVILEGE OF BEING CALLED BY HIS NAME

If you are insulted because you bear the name of Christ, you will be blessed, for the glorious Spirit of God rests upon you. If you suffer, however, it must not be for murder, stealing, making trouble, or prying into other people's affairs. But it is no shame to suffer for being a Christian. Praise God for the privilege of being called by his name!
1 PETER 4:14–16 NLT

The wounds from the words of others who ridicule you for your faith in Jesus can feel so painful and deep. But there is healing in the words of scripture: "God blesses you when people mock you and persecute you and lie about you and say all sorts of evil things against you because you are my followers. Be happy about it! Be very glad! For a great reward awaits you in heaven. And remember, the ancient prophets were persecuted in the same way" (Matthew 5:11–12 NLT).

Dear Jesus, I will follow You no matter what anyone says against me. I am so grateful for the privilege of being called Your follower—a Christian. I can't deny that words can hurt sometimes, though, so please remind me of Your promises. Heal my pain and help me to hold my head high as I put my hope in You! Amen.

Day 279

TAKE A BREAK

"Only in returning to me and resting in me will you be saved."
Isaiah 30:15 nlt

Some days you try everything you can think of to save yourself, but no matter how hard you try, you fail again and again. You fall on your face and embarrass yourself. You hurt the people around you. You make mistakes, and nothing whatsoever seems to go right. When that happens, it's time to take a break. You need to stop trying so hard. Throw yourself in God's arms. Rest on His grace, knowing that He will save you.

Father, sometimes I feel so unsure of myself. Help me to relax, to rest in Your arms, and to remember that You are my good teacher, my support, and my comfort. Amen.

CELESTIAL THANKSGIVING

*And all the angels stood round about the throne. . .
and fell before the throne on their faces, and worshipped
God, saying, Amen: Blessing, and glory, and wisdom,
and thanksgiving, and honour, and power, and
might, be unto our God for ever and ever. Amen.*
REVELATION 7:11–12 KJV

Over and over again throughout the Bible, we are reminded
to be filled with gratitude, to offer up thanksgiving to the God
who has blessed us so richly. But gratitude is not only a human
characteristic that draws us closer to God; it is also something
that flows through all creation. When John had his amazing
revelation of heaven, he saw the angels there falling on their
faces and singing songs of thanksgiving. So when we too lift our
voices in gratitude to God for all He has done, we are joining
in the angels' song! We are becoming part of heaven's endless
anthem of praise.

*Remind me, Father God, that when I give You
thanks, I am joining my heart with the angels.*

OUR WORK FOR THE LORD

*I thank Christ Jesus our Lord, who has given
me strength to do his work. He considered me
trustworthy and appointed me to serve him.*
1 TIMOTHY 1:12 NLT

God calls each of us to some work. That God-given work may
find its expression in our careers (the jobs that pay us money),
but it may also extend far beyond our nine-to-five employment.
This work is uniquely suited to each of us; no one else could do
it as well or the same. It is one of the reasons God created us,
and it is meant to give us as much joy as it does others. Whether
it's cooking meals for those who need them, lending a listening
ear to those who are troubled, writing grant proposals for a
nonprofit organization in need of funds, helping people with
their taxes, or painting beautiful images, God uses our work
to build His kingdom.

*Christ Jesus, help me to remember that the work You have
given me is one more reason for me to thank You.*

GOD KNIT YOU TOGETHER

For you created my inmost being; you knit me together in my mother's womb. I praise you because I am fearfully and wonderfully made; your works are wonderful, I know that full well. My frame was not hidden from you when I was made in the secret place, when I was woven together in the depths of the earth. Your eyes saw my unformed body; all the days ordained for me were written in your book before one of them came to be.

PSALM 139:13–16 NIV

No one knows you better than the one true Creator God who made you. He planned you and all the days of your life before you were even born. The God of all the universe put every piece of you together, and He loves you most and wants what's best for you in all things. Since all these things are true, don't ever let anyone put you down or steal your hope.

Heavenly Father, when I start to lose hope and feel discouraged, please help me not to forget that You designed me and the plans for my life in great detail and with great love. Amen.

HOPE LIKE THE POOR WIDOW

Jesus sat down near the collection box in the Temple and watched as the crowds dropped in their money. Many rich people put in large amounts. Then a poor widow came and dropped in two small coins. Jesus called his disciples to him and said, "I tell you the truth, this poor widow has given more than all the others who are making contributions. For they gave a tiny part of their surplus, but she, poor as she is, has given everything she had to live on."

MARK 12:41–44 NLT

Clearly, this poor widow had great hope and trust in God. Not many of us can say we would do the same as she and readily give God our last two pennies with total faith in His provision despite total uncertainty of what would come next. In the Christian faith, the humblest individuals are the true heroes. This poor widow is a role model for real hope in God—giving to Him and trusting Him to provide for our every need in every uncertainty.

Heavenly Father, help me to hope in You like the poor widow did. I want to be willing to give everything I have to You, trusting You to provide everything I need. Amen.

RIGHT NOW

For God says, "At just the right time, I heard you.
On the day of salvation, I helped you." Indeed, the
"right time" is now. Today is the day of salvation.
2 CORINTHIANS 6:2 NLT

God always meets us right now, in the present moment. We don't need to waste our time looking over our shoulders at the past, and we don't have to feel as though we need to reach some future moment before we can truly touch God. He is here now. Today, this very moment, is full of His grace.

Lord, make me mindful of Your presence right now, in this very minute. You have redeemed my past, and You hold my future in Your hands. This moment is the one I must cling to. Amen.

GOD IS ALWAYS THERE

Where can I go from your Spirit? Where can I flee from your presence? If I go up to the heavens, you are there; if I make my bed in the depths, you are there. If I rise on the wings of the dawn, if I settle on the far side of the sea, even there your hand will guide me, your right hand will hold me fast. If I say, "Surely the darkness will hide me and the light become night around me," even the darkness will not be dark to you; the night will shine like the day, for darkness is as light to you.

PSALM 139:7–12 NIV

No matter how hard or painful your circumstance, you are never alone in it. God's presence, through His Holy Spirit, never leaves you. As hard as it is for our minds to comprehend it, He is omnipresent—everywhere at all times. He knows your every thought, hears your every cry, sees your every tear. He will hold your hand and guide you. So keep your hope in Him and don't let go.

Heavenly Father, I trust You are here with me right in this moment and in every moment through Your Holy Spirit. You know my hardship and pain. I trust that Your hand is guiding me through it. I won't let go. Amen.

CAPABLE HANDS

Surely he shall not be moved for ever: the righteous shall be in everlasting remembrance. He shall not be afraid of evil tidings: his heart is fixed, trusting in the LORD. His heart is established, he shall not be afraid, until he see his desire upon his enemies.

PSALM 112:6–8 KJV

———

We live in uncertain times—economically, politically, and globally. Yet you can greet each new day with your head held high, confident and unafraid. Why? Because you have a God who cares deeply about you and the world around you. When your confidence is placed firmly in God instead of your own abilities, bank account, or "good karma," you need not fear the future. It's in God's powerful, capable, and compassionate hands.

I put my full trust in You, Lord! All my times are in Your hands. I've seen You take care of me every day of my life, and I trust that You will always hold me close.

MAKER OF MOUNTAINS

*For the LORD is the one who shaped the mountains, stirs up
the winds, and reveals his thoughts to mankind. He turns
the light of dawn into darkness and treads on the heights of
the earth. The LORD God of Heaven's Armies is his name!*
AMOS 4:13 NLT

Time in the mountains is both peaceful and overwhelming—
the mountains remind us how incredibly small and weak we
humans are in comparison to the size and strength of such
majestic landforms. Can you imagine God easily walking around
on top of them? The Bible says He can! When you are facing
problems or fears that seem like mountains that are far too
massive for you to handle, picture the Lord God of All walking
on top of them and then reaching down His hand to help you
over them.

*Heavenly Father, You are great and mighty! You are
able to help me overcome any problems that might
seem like unmoving mountains in my life. Please keep
holding my hand and helping me over them. Amen.*

Day 288

REJOICE IN CONFIDENT HOPE

Don't just pretend to love others. Really love them.
Hate what is wrong. Hold tightly to what is good.
Love each other with genuine affection, and take delight
in honoring each other. Never be lazy, but work hard and
serve the Lord enthusiastically. Rejoice in our confident
hope. Be patient in trouble, and keep on praying.
ROMANS 12:9–12 NLT

Paul's instructions here in Romans 12 sum up the Christian
life so well. We all need to compare our lives to this scripture
regularly. Are we truly loving other people? Hating what is
wrong? Holding tightly to what is good? Loving others with real
affection and delighting in honoring each other? Working hard
without laziness? Serving the Lord enthusiastically? Rejoicing
in confident hope? Being patient in trouble? Praying all the
time? Where your answers are *yes*, celebrate and worship God
for His grace in growing the fruit of the Spirit in you! Where
your answers are *no* or *need work*, admit your struggles to God
and ask for His help to improve.

Heavenly Father, please help me to live my life as You
have instructed in Your Word. Affirm and encourage
me in the ways I'm doing well, and correct me
where I need to change and improve. Amen.

PEACEFUL HEARTS

*You will keep in perfect peace all who trust in
you, all whose thoughts are fixed on you!*
Isaiah 26:3 NLT

Peace seems very far away sometimes. But it's not! Peace isn't
an emotion we can work up in our own strength. It's one of the
gifts of grace God longs to give us. All we need to do is focus
on Him. As we give Him all our worries, one by one, every day,
He will do His part: He will keep our hearts at peace.

*Jesus, I am incredibly grateful for Your peace. It is a gift I
need every moment of every day. When my heart gets anxious,
comfort me with the peace only You can provide. Amen.*

SHAKY TIMES

*Therefore, since we are receiving a kingdom that
cannot be shaken, let us be thankful, and so worship
God acceptably with reverence and awe.*
HEBREWS 12:28 NIV

We live in a shaky world. Pandemics, protests, and politics
have made all of us feel a little wobbly. We fret about what will
happen next. We worry about our children and other loved
ones. Often we feel helpless and anxious—maybe even terrified
at times. But even though our world has its share of financial,
societal, and spiritual earthquakes, we need to remember that
we also inhabit the kingdom of God—and *that* kingdom can
never be shaken. No matter what happens in the world, we can
continue to be thankful and at peace, knowing we are truly
citizens of another world, one that is unshakable.

**Thank You, Lord God, that no matter
what happens, I am safe in You.**

HIS HEART OVERFLOWED WITH COMPASSION

A funeral procession was coming out as he approached the village gate. The young man who had died was a widow's only son, and a large crowd from the village was with her. When the Lord saw her, his heart overflowed with compassion. "Don't cry!" he said. Then he walked over to the coffin and touched it, and the bearers stopped. "Young man," he said, "I tell you, get up." Then the dead boy sat up and began to talk! And Jesus gave him back to his mother.

LUKE 7:12–15 NLT

In Bible times, if a woman had no husband and no sons, she was in a dangerous situation. It was nearly impossible for a woman to provide for herself and protect herself without a man back then. So when Jesus saw this widow whose son had just died, He had extra concern for her. "His heart overflowed with compassion." Then He brought her dead son back to life and gave him back to his mother. Can you imagine her extreme joy and relief and total awe and gratitude for Jesus?

Dear Jesus, thank You for Your miracles and Your compassion! You care so much about people who are in awful situations. Help me to trust in Your care, knowing that You can provide healing here on earth and, ultimately, healing in heaven forever. Help me also to care for others like You do. Amen.

VALUABLE

*Better to be patient than powerful; better to
have self-control than to conquer a city.*
PROVERBS 16:32 NLT

Our world values visible power. We appreciate things like
prestige and skill, wealth and influence. But God looks at
things differently. From His perspective, the quiet and easily
overlooked quality of patience is far more valuable than any
worldly power. Patience makes room for others' needs and
brokenness. Patience creates a space in our lives for God's
grace to flow through us.

*Lord, when I come to Your Word, I am constantly reminded
that Your wisdom is not the world's wisdom. Give me Your
perspective. Draw me toward the practice of patience. Amen.*

PAST, PRESENT, AND FUTURE

We give thee thanks, O LORD God Almighty,
which art, and wast, and art to come.

REVELATION 11:17 KJV

Psychologists have noted that the human brain has a hard time resting in the present moment. Instead, we tend to either obsess about the past or drive ourselves crazy worrying about the future. God wants to meet us right here, in this present moment. We may miss out on what He is doing *now* when we are preoccupied by the past or the future. But we can rest assured that whether our minds are focused on the past, the present, or the future, God is right there. We can thank Him that He is a past, present, and future God.

Lord God Almighty, thank You that You were there in my past; thank You that You are here in this present moment; and thank You that You will be with me in the future, all the way to eternity.

YOUR STRENGTH AND REFUGE

But as for me, I will sing about your power. Each morning I will sing with joy about your unfailing love. For you have been my refuge, a place of safety when I am in distress. O my Strength, to you I sing praises, for you, O God, are my refuge, the God who shows me unfailing love.
PSALM 59:16–17 NLT

Nothing ever compares to God as your ultimate source of strength and refuge. His power is far beyond any kind of human strength. When you choose to focus on it and even sing about it in praise and worship, you can be filled with great hope and courage. You can remember that you never need to depend on your own strength when you have God with you. He will not fail you.

Heavenly Father, my strength and refuge, I love You and praise You and put my hope in You. I know You are strong enough to do anything to help whenever I need it. Amen.

TRUE CONTENTMENT

The Lord is my shepherd; I shall not want.
Psalm 23:1 KJV

When it comes to brains, sheep are not the sharpest crayons in the box. They frighten easily, tend to follow the crowd, and have limited abilities for defending themselves. That's why sheep thrive best with a shepherd who guides, protects, and cares for their needs. Our Good Shepherd will do the same for us. Worry, fear, and discontent are products of a sheepish mentality. However, the peace of true contentment can be ours when we follow God's lead.

Like sheep who know their master's voice, teach me to hear from You, Lord. I trust You to take care of my needs. Help me to follow You wherever You lead.

HOPE BECAUSE OF FRIENDSHIP

Two people are better off than one, for they can help each other succeed. If one person falls, the other can reach out and help. But someone who falls alone is in real trouble. Likewise, two people lying close together can keep each other warm. But how can one be warm alone? A person standing alone can be attacked and defeated, but two can stand back-to-back and conquer. Three are even better, for a triple-braided cord is not easily broken.
ECCLESIASTES 4:9–12 NLT

Friendship is so important to encourage us and bring us hope. It's one of God's greatest gifts! In friendship, we help each other and support each other and protect each other and stand against enemies together too. Plus, it's just so much fun to have good friends to spend time with and laugh with! That's God's extra-special blessing on top. He gives us so much joy through good friendships. What a wonderful heavenly Father we have!

Heavenly Father, thank You for the gift of good friendships that encourage me and fill me with hope and love and joy! Please help my friends and me grow closer to each other and, most of all, closer to You! Amen.

Day 297

HE IS RISEN!

Then the angel spoke to the women. "Don't be afraid!"
he said. "I know you are looking for Jesus, who was
crucified. He isn't here! He is risen from the dead, just as
he said would happen. Come, see where his body was lying.
And now, go quickly and tell his disciples that he has risen
from the dead, and he is going ahead of you to Galilee.
You will see him there. Remember what I have told you."
MATTHEW 28:5–9 NLT

Can you imagine being one of these women, these dear friends of Jesus? It had to be the most wonderful surprise ever to hear the angel's news and then meet up with Jesus who was not dead but alive again! That powerful news is what we still trust today. Jesus is not dead. He is alive!

Dear Jesus, I believe You died to save me from my sin,
but You did not stay dead. You are alive! You are my
hope and the hope of the whole world. Amen.

HOPE IN THE MIDST OF FEAR AND ANXIETY

God gave us a spirit not of fear but of power and love and self-control.
2 TIMOTHY 1:7 ESV

When fear and anxiety are creeping up on you, what good and healthy things help calm you down and comfort you and make you feel safe? Bible verses you've memorized should be a top go-to, like 2 Timothy 1:7, reminding you that God has given you a spirit of power, love, and self-control to defeat any spirit of fear. Another to memorize and repeat is Psalm 56:3–4 (NLV): "When I am afraid, I will trust in You. I praise the Word of God. I have put my trust in God. I will not be afraid." God's Word is powerful to help us when we feel anxiety and fear.

Heavenly Father, thank You for Your Word that I can remember and repeat when I need to focus on Your power and love. Please take my anxiety and fear and replace them with Your hope and peace. Amen.

Day 299

HEALED PAST

*"All their past sins will be forgotten, and they will live
because of the righteous things they have done."*
Ezekiel 18:22 nlt

We have the feeling that we can't do anything about the past.
We think all our mistakes are back there behind us, carved in
stone. But God's creative power is amazing, and His grace can
heal even the past. Yesterday's sins are pulled out like weeds,
while the good things we have done are watered so that they
grow and flourish into the present. Give your past to God.
His grace is big enough to bring healing even to your worst
memories.

*Father, how grateful I am that my past is forgiven
and that I am free! Help me to continue to trust
You to bring righteousness into my life. Amen.*

BIG ENOUGH

Out of them shall proceed thanksgiving and the voice of them that make merry: and I will multiply them, and they shall not be few; I will also glorify them, and they shall not be small.
JEREMIAH 30:19 KJV

Do you ever feel small? Even though we are grown-ups with adult responsibilities, most of us have at least a little piece inside of us that never quite grew up. That inner child can be a source of joy and fun but also can make us feel too little to cope with life's challenges. God wants to bless that child, though, and one of the ways we allow Him to do that is by making gratitude a habit. As we practice thanksgiving daily, He fills us with light. We will still be able to laugh and play like a child—"make merry," as the King James Version says—but we will also be big enough to take on the work God has ordained for us.

Thank You, God, that Your love lifts me up, strengthens me, and makes me big enough to face the challenges of my life.

Day 301

TRAIN FOR GODLINESS

Train yourself for godliness; for while bodily training is of some value, godliness is of value in every way, as it holds promise for the present life and also for the life to come. The saying is trustworthy and deserving of full acceptance. For to this end we toil and strive, because we have our hope set on the living God, who is the Savior of all people, especially of those who believe.
1 TIMOTHY 4:7–10 ESV

Struggling to maintain good health in an aging body in a world that glamorizes top physical fitness can make you feel hopeless. Of course, we need to do our best to take good care of our bodies and health, but too many in our society worship physical fitness like a god. Ask God for wisdom and discipline for healthy living, eating, and exercise; but even more, ask God for wisdom and discipline for healthy training in godliness—spending time studying and learning God's Word and letting yourself be shaped by it, both for now and for eternity.

Heavenly Father, please help me with my physical health, but even more, please help me with my spiritual health. My hope is not in my earthly body. My hope is in You and the eternal life You promise. Amen.

WITH GOD, ALL THINGS ARE POSSIBLE

*Jesus said to his disciples, "Truly, I say to you, only with
difficulty will a rich person enter the kingdom of heaven.
Again I tell you, it is easier for a camel to go through
the eye of a needle than for a rich person to enter the
kingdom of God." When the disciples heard this, they were
greatly astonished, saying, "Who then can be saved?"
But Jesus looked at them and said, "With man this is
impossible, but with God all things are possible."*
MATTHEW 19:23–26 ESV

Maybe you are praying for someone you love to trust in Jesus
as their Savior, but they keep refusing to admit their need for
Him. Their salvation might seem absolutely impossible, but
keep on hoping and praying for them and loving them anyway.
Remember the promise in these words of Jesus from Matthew
19 that "with God all things are possible."

*Heavenly Father, I pray for my friends and loved ones
who seem so unwilling to trust in You as Savior. Help me
to remember that nothing is impossible for You! Amen.*

THRIVE!

Those who trust in their riches will fall,
but the righteous will thrive like a green leaf.
PROVERBS 11:28 NIV

Money seems so important in our world. Many things we want depend on money—that remodeling project we're hoping to do, the Christmas gifts we want to give, the vacation we hope to take, and the new car we want to drive. There's nothing wrong with any of those things, but our enjoyment of them will always be fleeting. Only God's daily grace makes us truly grow and thrive.

Father, remind me that while caring for my family,
making money, and preparing for my future are
good things, they are not my identity. Help me to
find my purpose, my worth, in You. Amen.

SLEEPLESS NIGHTS

At midnight I rise to give you thanks.
PSALM 119:62 NIV

We may not want to set our alarms to wake us in the middle of the night for a prayer session with God (though it might not be a bad idea to do that from time to time!), but there are nights that find us lying awake as the minutes and then hours tick past. When sleep won't come, it's easy to find ourselves going over all our worries, magnifying them until they loom over us and our hearts beat faster with anxiety. But we have other options. On those nights when insomnia overtakes us, we can use the wakeful hours to turn to God in gratitude. Instead of counting sheep, we can count our blessings—and as thanksgiving fills our hearts, we may find ourselves relaxing into sleep.

Lord, when sleep won't come, remind me to turn my worries into thanksgiving for all Your blessings.

HOPE FOR SOMETHING NEW

"But forget all that—it is nothing compared to what I am going to do. For I am about to do something new. See, I have already begun! Do you not see it? I will make a pathway through the wilderness. I will create rivers in the dry wasteland."
ISAIAH 43:18–19 NLT

In this scripture, God was telling His people to forget the hard times of the past and let Him bring them into something new and good. Do you have hard times you need to forget too? We all do. Maybe you feel like last year was just awful, and now you feel worried about the new year ahead. But just be glad last year (or whatever it is that you're glad is over) is done, and let it go! Let God help you every moment of every day. Let His wonderful grace cover you and His amazing love, joy, and peace fill you up. Let Him restore your hope. Let Him protect you and lead you. Let Him do the new things He wants to do in and through you.

Heavenly Father, help me to focus with great hope and confidence on the awesome new things You are doing. You are in me, and my life is from You and for You. Please fill me up with Your good blessings. Amen.

REPETITION

Give thanks to the LORD, for he is good! His faithful love endures forever. Give thanks to the God of gods. His faithful love endures forever. Give thanks to the Lord of lords. His faithful love endures forever. Give thanks to him who alone does mighty miracles. His faithful love endures forever. Give thanks to him who made the heavens so skillfully. His faithful love endures forever. . . . Give thanks to the God of heaven. His faithful love endures forever.

PSALM 136:1–5, 26 NLT

The psalmist knew the secret of gratitude. He understood that thanksgiving never gets boring, no matter how many times it's repeated. In fact, with each expression of gratitude, our hearts expand, allowing God's Spirit to fill us ever more deeply. These verses from Psalm 136 are good ones to repeat throughout the day to remind us of God's faithful love that will endure forever.

You are so good, Lord. Your faithful love endures forever.

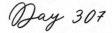
Day 307

WEB OF LOVE

*So now I am giving you a new commandment: Love each
other. Just as I have loved you, you should love each other.*
JOHN 13:34 NLT

God's grace comes to us through a net of relationships and
connections. Because we know we are totally and unconditionally loved, we can in turn love others. The connections
between us grow ever wider and stronger, a web of love that
unites us all with God.

*Jesus, I am grateful for the relationships You have
given me. Thank You for Your love that enables
me to love and be loved by others. Amen.*

CULTIVATE CONTENTMENT

*Surely I have behaved and quieted myself, as a child that is
weaned of his mother: my soul is even as a weaned child.*
PSALM 131:2 KJV

Picture a well-fed newborn resting in her mother's arms, peacefully gazing up into her eyes. That's contentment. No worrying about "Does this diaper make me look fat?" No fears over "Will social security be around when I retire?" No burning desire for a nicer stroller or a bigger crib. Allow God to baby you. Gaze into His eyes by recalling the ways He's provided for you. Cultivate contentment by trusting Him as a mother is trusted by her child.

*Your Word tells me that as a mother comforts her child,
so will You comfort me, Lord. I accept Your comfort. I
want that in my life. Draw me close to You, Father.*

HOPE FROM ANGELS

*Are not all the angels spirits who work for
God? They are sent out to help those who are
to be saved from the punishment of sin.*
HEBREWS 1:14 NLV

Do you think much about angels? It's important that what
we believe about them comes not from the world's ideas but
from the truth in God's Word. This scripture shows us that we
can trust that angels absolutely exist, and we can put hope
in how they will minister to us. They are spirits who work
for God, and they are sent to help all who trust in Jesus as
Savior from their sin. The fact of their existence and mission
is amazing to think about! We can confidently ask God to send
His angels to care for us and rescue us and others from any
kind of trouble.

*Heavenly Father, thank You that angels are real. Please send
them to me when I need them. Thank You for the ways You care
for me and protect me through the help of angels. Amen.*

HOPE IN THE MIDST OF UNCERTAINTY

*Confused and disturbed, Mary tried to
think what the angel could mean.*
LUKE 1:29 NLT

Imagine being Mary—the shock of suddenly becoming miraculously pregnant after being told by an angel that she had been chosen to carry the Son of God! Mary could have given in to anxiety and fear, but instead she chose hope and praise and a humble willingness to be used by God however He led. Mary's response—"I am the Lord's servant. May everything you have said about me come true" (Luke 1:38 NLT)—and her song found in Luke 1:46–55 inspire all of us to cling to hope in the midst of great uncertainty. May we say, no matter our circumstances, "Oh, how my soul praises the Lord. How my spirit rejoices in God my Savior!" (verses 46–47 NLT).

*Heavenly Father, no matter what You ask me to do in life,
no matter how hard it might be, I want to have the kind
of response Mary had. Please help me. I want to be willing
to do anything for You—and praise You through all of it.
I know You are good and ask only good things of me. Amen.*

SING!

*But each day the LORD pours his unfailing love
upon me, and through each night I sing his
songs, praying to God who gives me life.*
PSALM 42:8 NLT

Life itself is a gift of grace. The very blood that flows through our veins, the beat of our hearts, and the steady hum of our metabolism—all of that is God's free gift to us, a token of His constant and unconditional love. When we are so richly loved, how can we help but sing, even in the darkness?

*Dear Lord, giver of blessing and giver of life, as I
experience Your unfailing love each and every day,
teach my heart to sing Your joyful song. Amen.*

GOD DID NOT ABANDON THEM

"But our ancestors were proud and stubborn, and they paid no attention to your commands. They refused to obey and did not remember the miracles you had done for them. . . . But you are a God of forgiveness, gracious and merciful, slow to become angry, and rich in unfailing love. You did not abandon them, even when they made an idol shaped like a calf and said, 'This is your god who brought you out of Egypt!' They committed terrible blasphemies. But in your great mercy you did not abandon them."

NEHEMIAH 9:16–19 NLT

Be reminded by God's Word of how patient and good our God is, even when His people treat Him horribly. Even then, He is forgiving and kind and loving. He provides for His people and gives us His Holy Spirit to teach us. This scripture might be about ancient times and ancient people, but we can apply the truth in it to our own lives today.

Heavenly Father, knowing that You don't abandon Your people fills me with hope. Thank You for Your amazing grace and compassionate mercy. Amen.

Day 313

LAUGH OUT LOUD

*"He will once again fill your mouth with
laughter and your lips with shouts of joy."*
JOB 8:21 NLT

Did you know that God wants to make you laugh? He wants
to fill you with loud, rowdy joy. Oh, some days His grace will
come to you quietly and calmly. But every now and then, you
will have days when He makes you laugh out loud.

*Heavenly Father, the gift of laughter is such
a blessing. Help me to look for reasons to
laugh out loud with Your joy. Amen.*

WELL EQUIPPED

*Put on the full armor of God, so that when the day of evil
comes, you may be able to stand your ground, and after you
have done everything, to stand. Stand firm then, with the
belt of truth buckled around your waist, with the breastplate
of righteousness in place, and with your feet fitted with the
readiness that comes from the gospel of peace. In addition to all
this, take up the shield of faith, with which you can extinguish
all the flaming arrows of the evil one. Take the helmet of
salvation and the sword of the Spirit, which is the word of God.*
EPHESIANS 6:13–17 NIV

God knows we will have battles in this world—battles with
our enemy the devil and the spiritual forces of evil. But God
never leaves us helpless or hopeless in these battles. We have
the Holy Spirit in us, and He gives us armor and weapons to be
protected and ready to fight! Think about these verses when
you feel under attack, and remember God will never let the
devil defeat you.

*Heavenly Father, thank You for equipping me in every battle
against evil. I am strong and able to fight because of You! Amen.*

GOODNESS AND MERCY
ALL YOUR DAYS

Surely goodness and mercy shall follow me all the days of my life, and I shall dwell in the house of the LORD forever.

PSALM 23:6 ESV

The psalmist David didn't say *only* goodness and mercy would follow him all his days. But he did say they *would* follow him. And they will follow you today as well, even in whatever struggle or pain or illness you are going through. As you endure hardship, look specifically for the goodness and mercy you see in each day, even when heartache and confusion and suffering are raging at their worst. Cling to that goodness and mercy. Write it down. Pray in gratitude for it. Sing praise about it. Remember it tomorrow even while you look for the new goodness and mercy and grace God will give you. He will carry you through, until one day you are dwelling in His house forever.

Heavenly Father, help me to notice and appreciate each and every bit of goodness and mercy You are constantly giving me, even in the midst of trials. I praise you and thank You for it all, and I trust in You to continue to give it. Amen.

WAS IT AN ANGEL?

"Last night an angel of the God to whom I belong and whom I serve stood beside me, and he said, 'Don't be afraid, Paul.'"
ACTS 27:23–24 NLT

Has a stranger ever said something to you that was exactly what you needed to hear? Maybe someone comforted you. Maybe someone reassured and encouraged you. What if that someone was really an angel sent by God? It really could have been, especially if you'd never seen the person before and you've never seen them since! Whenever you have an experience like that, notice and thank God for it. Whether it was an angel or not, God used that someone in your life to help you. You can trust that He will always send the right people or angels to you with exactly the right words and help exactly when you need them.

Heavenly Father, thank You for the times You have used people I don't even know to help me and encourage me. You give hope and help through all kinds of people and in all kinds of ways. Amen.

WHAT GOD SHOWS US

*The LORD is righteous in everything he
does; he is filled with kindness.*
PSALM 145:17 NLT

Did you know that the word *kind* comes from the same root
as *kin*? Both words originally had to do with intimate shared
relationships like the ones that exist between members of the
same family. This is what God shows us: the kindness of a good
father, the gentleness of a good mother, the understanding of
a brother or sister.

*Good Father, thank You for Your kindness and
for creating me with a longing to be close to You.
May I find rest in Your nearness. Amen.*

BOLD AND COURAGEOUS

In the day when I cried thou answeredst me,
and strengthenedst me with strength in my soul.
PSALM 138:3 KJV

Women are often characterized as timid creatures—fleeing from spiders, screaming over mice, cowering behind big, burly men when danger is near. But the Bible characterizes women of God as bold and courageous. Queen Esther risked her life to save God's children from genocide. Deborah led an army and judged the tribes of Israel. Rahab dared to hide Jewish spies to save her family. Today, God will supply the courage you need to accomplish whatever He's asked you to do.

Please fill me with boldness and courage that comes from You alone, heavenly Father. I don't want to be known for my own strength but for what You have done through me.

GIVE GOD ALL THE CREDIT AND PRAISE

If anyone wants to be proud, he should be proud of what the Lord has done. It is not what a man thinks and says of himself that is important. It is what God thinks of him.
2 Corinthians 10:17–18 nlv

Our hope and pride should never be in ourselves and our own accomplishments. Of course, we feel happy when we achieve or complete something great. And that's wonderful! But we must never forget to always give God credit for each good thing we do. He deserves every bit of praise and worship because He is the one who gives us all our gifts and abilities.

Heavenly Father, please help me never to hope or have pride in myself but rather remember You are the one who gives me every reason to feel proud and have hope. Every good thing comes from You, and You are so generous! I'm so grateful! Amen.

GOD WILL NEVER LEAVE YOU OR LET YOU BE ALONE

God has said, "I will never leave you or let you be alone." So we can say for sure, "The Lord is my Helper. I am not afraid of anything man can do to me."
HEBREWS 13:5–6 NLV

Being alone during a difficult time can make the situation feel practically unbearable. But to have even just one friend or loved one by your side devotedly can make all the difference in the world. Praise God for those precious people! Yet there are times in life when we have to do some difficult things without another person by our side for support. Even then, however, we are never truly alone because of the Holy Spirit within us. God has promised He never leaves us and never lets us be alone. He knows our situation and every thought and fear and need. He hears our every prayer. And He will answer in amazing ways to always show Himself as our helper.

Heavenly Father, I believe You never leave me or let me be alone. Thank You for those times when You provide dear people to stay right by my side supporting me. And thank You for those times when You provide supernatural comfort and companionship. I'm grateful for Your constant presence in my life. Amen.

PRAYING FOR EVERYONE

I urge you, first of all, to pray for all people. Ask God to help them; intercede on their behalf, and give thanks for them.
1 TIMOTHY 2:1 NLT

Most of us pray for the people who are important to us, our family and friends we love so much—but in this verse, the Bible is telling us to pray for *all* people. That includes people we don't know personally, such as people we've heard about in the news. Whenever we read or watch a news story, we can make a habit of saying a prayer for the individuals concerned. The instruction to pray for all people also includes people we don't like. It includes people who do bad things. And not only are we told to lift them up to God, asking that He would bless them and help them, but we are also told to give thanks for them. This is the radical gratitude that reaches out beyond our selfishness and embraces the entire world.

Jesus, friend of all humanity, teach me to love as You love. May my prayers of intercession and gratitude not only bless others but also draw me ever closer to You.

A STATE OF GRATITUDE

*Jesus then took the loaves, gave thanks, and
distributed to those who were seated as much as
they wanted. He did the same with the fish.*
JOHN 6:11 NIV

In this verse, Jesus is modeling for us how we are to behave when we receive a gift, no matter how small. A crowd of hungry people surrounded Jesus, and the only food anyone had offered to share was a small boy's lunch. But Jesus did not dismiss the gift as being so meager as to be useless. Instead, the original language in which this account was written reports that Jesus was in a "state of gratitude." He was thankful for what had been given to Him, even though it was small—and then He shared it with everyone else gathered around Him. When we too learn to be thankful for even the smallest gifts and learn to share what we have been given with others, who knows how God may choose to bless us?

*Jesus, teach me to be more like You. May I learn
to live my life in a state of gratitude.*

INTO GOD'S PRESENCE

"That person can pray to God and find favor with him, they will see God's face and shout for joy."

JOB 33:26 NIV

Prayer is the channel through which God's grace flows. We do not pray because God needs us to pray; we pray because we need to pray. When we come into God's presence, we are renewed. Our hearts lift. We look into the face of the one who loves us most, and we are filled with joy.

Father, thank You for the gift of prayer and the promise that I can talk with You at any time. As I look to You, fill my heart with Your joy. Amen.

HOW SWEET IS GOD'S WORD

O, how I love Your Law! It is what I think about all through the day. Your Word makes me wiser than those who hate me, for it is always with me. I have better understanding than all my teachers because I think about Your Law. I have a better understanding than those who are old because I obey Your Word. I have kept my feet from every sinful way so that I may keep Your Word. I have not turned away from Your Law, for You Yourself have taught me. How sweet is Your Word to my taste! It is sweeter than honey to my mouth! I get understanding from Your Law and so I hate every false way.
PSALM 119:97–104 NLV

This scripture from Psalms shows how we should think of God's Word and praise Him for it. The Bible is living and active (Hebrews 4:12) and is inspired by God and useful in every area of our lives (2 Timothy 3:16). Like the psalmist, we should have great love and enthusiasm for God's Word, recognizing how blessed we are to learn from it, follow it, and receive hope from it, with the help of the Holy Spirit.

Heavenly Father, thank You for the gift of Your Word! Help me to value it the way I should. Remind me of this psalm every day. I sing and pray it to You right now with all of my heart. Amen.

Day 325

DEEP ROOTS

As you have put your trust in Christ Jesus the Lord to save you from the punishment of sin, now let Him lead you in every step. Have your roots planted deep in Christ. Grow in Him. Get your strength from Him. Let Him make you strong in the faith as you have been taught. Your life should be full of thanks to Him.
COLOSSIANS 2:6–7 NLV

How strong is your faith in Christ? Can it always get stronger? Absolutely! As you let Him lead you in every step through the work of the Holy Spirit, your roots will grow deeper and deeper into Him. The deeper the roots of a tree go, the stronger it is. The deeper its roots grow, the harder it is for the tree to fall. The same goes for you. The deeper your roots grow in Jesus, the stronger you are in your faith and the harder it is for any difficult thing in life to make you fall.

Dear Jesus, please keep me growing deeper roots into You. Strengthen my faith each day as You lead me in every step. Amen.

THINKING HABITS

And now, dear brothers and sisters, one final thing.
Fix your thoughts on what is true, and honorable, and
right, and pure, and lovely, and admirable. Think about
things that are excellent and worthy of praise.
PHILIPPIANS 4:8 NLT

Our brains are gifts from God, intended to serve us well, special gifts of grace we often take for granted. In return, we need to offer our minds back to God. Practice thinking positive thoughts. Focus on what is true rather than on lies; pay attention to beautiful things and stop staring at the ugly things in life. Discipline your minds to take on God's habits of thinking.

Heavenly Father, thank You for my brain, a gift
from You. Help me focus on things that honor
You. Open my eyes to beautiful, positive things—
and most importantly to Your truth. Amen.

Day 327

OPPORTUNE TIME

Wait on the LORD: be of good courage, and he shall strengthen thine heart: wait, I say, on the LORD.
PSALM 27:14 KJV

Foolhardiness can look like courage at first glance. However, true courage counts the cost before it forges ahead. If you're faced with a risky decision, it's not only wise to think before you act, it's biblical. Ecclesiastes 3:1 (KJV) reminds us, "To every thing there is a season, and a time to every purpose under the heaven." Waiting for that right time takes patience and courage. Don't simply pray for courage. Pray for the wisdom to discern that "opportune time."

Father, I'm asking for wisdom again. I want to sit in Your presence as You fill me with Your power and presence. Show me how and when to act on Your promptings.

JESUS GIVES US PEACE

*"Peace I leave with you. My peace I give to you.
I do not give peace to you as the world gives.
Do not let your hearts be troubled or afraid."*

JOHN 14:27 NLV

Don't let the troubles of the world make you feel hopeless about ever having any peace. Jesus has given you a supernatural peace that transcends all understanding (Philippians 4:6–7). Peaceful things here on earth—a relaxing beach, a quiet afternoon, a laid-back get-together with family and friends—sure are nice, but they are not the deep, constant, miraculous peace that only Jesus can give. Whenever you feel troubled or afraid, ask the Holy Spirit to fill you with the perfect peace of Jesus.

Dear Jesus, anytime I am troubled or afraid, please calm me down by reminding me of Your perfect peace. Amen.

LESSONS FROM HABAKKUK

This is the special word which Habakkuk the man of God saw.
O Lord, how long must I call for help before You will hear?
I cry out to You, "We are being hurt!" But You do not save us.
HABAKKUK 1:1–2 NLV

We can all relate to asking God questions and feeling confused. Sometimes we wonder why we have to wait so long on Him or why He doesn't answer our prayers the way we hoped. Habakkuk was a prophet of God who had a lot of questions. We can learn from him that even though he never got the exact answers he wanted from God, he got answers that reminded him of this: God is all-powerful and completely good, and He will work out His perfect plans in His perfect timing. We must continue to trust what Habakkuk learned.

Heavenly Father, like Habakkuk, even when I have
questions and feel confused, I want to be able to say,
"Yet I will have joy in the Lord. I will be glad in the
God Who saves me" (Habakkuk 3:18 NLV). Amen.

NO OUTSIDERS

One of them, when he saw he was healed, came back,
praising God in a loud voice. He threw himself at Jesus' feet
and thanked him—and he was a Samaritan. Jesus asked,
"Were not all ten cleansed? Where are the other nine? Has no
one returned to give praise to God except this foreigner?" Then
he said to him, "Rise and go; your faith has made you well."
LUKE 17:15–19 NIV

In Jesus' day, Jews considered Samaritans to be outsiders. They
were scorned, looked down on, and thought to be less worthy
than the Jews. They were also thought to be dangerous, the
sort of people good Jews tried to avoid. In the story of the ten
lepers, Jesus makes clear that His blessings are for all people,
not just the people who look like us, speak like us, or worship
God like us. It may even be that the people we consider to be
"outsiders" have a deeper grasp of God than we do. We may
need to open our hearts so that we can learn about thankfulness and humility from those who understand these qualities
better than we do.

Show me, Jesus, any secret prejudices I've hidden away
in my heart. Give me a heart that is humble enough to be
open and grateful enough to never forget to thank You.

GRACE OF HOSPITALITY

When God's people are in need, be ready to help them. Always be eager to practice hospitality.
ROMANS 12:13 NLT

God opens Himself to you and offers you everything He has, and He calls you to do the same for others. Just as He made you welcome, make others welcome in your life. Don't reach out to others grudgingly, with a sense of obligation. Instead, be eager for opportunities to practice the grace of hospitality.

Father, although I long to help others in need, I can sure find a lot of excuses to avoid practicing hospitality. Please give me an eagerness to share with others. Amen.

LET YOURSELF LAMENT

*I have cried until the tears no longer come;
my heart is broken. My spirit is poured out in agony
as I see the desperate plight of my people.*

LAMENTATIONS 2:11 NLT

In the book of Lamentations, Jeremiah wrote down all of his sadness and pain over the destruction of the city of Jerusalem resulting from the people's turning away from God. The word *lamentation* means an expression of sorrow. For healing from heartache, we also might find it helpful to write down our feelings, telling God all about them and allowing Him to comfort and strengthen us again. We might want to share our lamentation with trusted loved ones as well, because God can use their care to help us.

*Heavenly Father, help me to remember it's okay
to acknowledge my feelings of heartache. Help me
to share them with You and with people who love
me. I trust that You will bring me the comfort and
encouragement and healing and hope I need. Amen.*

Day 333

A RICH LIFE

He has made your lives rich in every way. Now you have power to speak for Him. He gave you good understanding. This shows that what I told you about Christ and what He could do for you has been done in your lives. You have the gifts of the Holy Spirit that you need while you wait for the Lord Jesus Christ to come again. Christ will keep you strong until He comes again.

1 CORINTHIANS 1:5–8 NLV

What are the many ways God has made your life "rich in every way"? Do you have a gratitude journal in which to list them and focus on them? Thanking and praising God for His goodness to you fills you with hope for more of His goodness. Ask Him to show you the gifts of the Holy Spirit that He has given you. Let Him tell you how He wants you to use them specifically in this world until He comes again. Jesus knows you and loves you and will keep you strong until the day He returns!

Heavenly Father, thank You for making me rich in every way. Please keep me strong and help me to use these riches You have given me in the ways You want me to. Amen.

Day 334

EATING

Whoever eats meat does so to the Lord, for they give thanks to God; and whoever abstains does so to the Lord and gives thanks to God.

ROMANS 14:6 NIV

We live in a culture that is constantly telling us to diet. "Eat less so you'll be thin" is the message everywhere we turn. "Follow this special diet, and you'll lose that weight that's keeping you from being attractive." That message is hard to resist, and it makes our relationship with food complicated. God does want us to be healthy, and the Bible says that gluttony is a sin against the body just as much as any other unhealthy habit. But this verse from the book of Romans reminds us that God wants to heal our relationship with food. If He has called us to reduce our calories, we can do so with thanksgiving—and when we eat, we can also do so with thanksgiving.

Father God, heal my relationship with food.
Show me what is healthy for me. And may I always eat
with gratitude that You have given me enough.

Day 335

UNCHANGED

*Why am I discouraged? Why is my heart
so sad? I will put my hope in God!*
PSALM 42:5 NLT

Thousands of years ago, the psalmist who wrote these words expressed the same feelings we all have. Some days we just feel blue. The world looks dark, everything seems to be going wrong, and our hearts are sad. Those feelings are part of the human condition. Like the psalmist, we need to remind ourselves that God is unchanged by cloudy skies and gloomy hearts. His grace is always the same, as bright and hopeful as ever.

Heavenly Father, when I am overcome by sadness, help me to see Your light shimmering just beyond the clouds. Thank You for Your grace, which is a bright promise and a great comfort. Amen.

DAILY WALK

Keep back thy servant also from presumptuous sins;
let them not have dominion over me: then shall I be upright,
and I shall be innocent from the great transgression.

PSALM 19:13 KJV

Yesterday is over. Today is a brand-new day. Any mistakes or bad choices you've made in the past are behind you. God doesn't hold them against you. He's wiped your past clean with the power of forgiveness. The only thing left for you to do with the past is learn from it. Celebrate each new day by giving thanks to God for what He's done and by actively anticipating what He's going to do with the clean slate of today.

Father, thank You that Your mercies are new every morning!
I couldn't stand up under the burden of carrying my past
around with me. Thank You for a brand-new life in Christ!

ASK FOR GOOD GIFTS

"Ask and it will be given to you; seek and you will find; knock and the door will be opened to you. For everyone who asks receives; the one who seeks finds; and to the one who knocks, the door will be opened. Which of you, if your son asks for bread, will give him a stone? Or if he asks for a fish, will give him a snake? If you, then, though you are evil, know how to give good gifts to your children, how much more will your Father in heaven give good gifts to those who ask him!"

MATTHEW 7:7–11 NIV

God never tires of hearing of hearing from you (Romans 12:12; Ephesians 6:18; 1 Thessalonians 5:16–18). He's your wonderful heavenly Dad! His Word encourages you to pray about absolutely everything and ask Him to bless you. So keep talking to Him constantly! He loves you; He loves to listen to you; He loves to give you good things.

Heavenly Father, thank You for listening to me and giving me good gifts! Please bless me in the ways You know are best for me. Amen.

BE GENEROUS

"Give, and it will be given to you. You will have more than enough. It can be pushed down and shaken together and it will still run over as it is given to you. The way you give to others is the way you will receive in return."

LUKE 6:38 NLV

We are called to share God's love and hope with others by being generous. It takes courage to give away what we have to those in need, because we have to trust that we will still have what we need too. But there's no need to fret. God will always supply enough for our own needs as we help provide for the needs of others. The Bible promises it! The more we give, the more God will give us! He loves to reward us when we share the gifts that ultimately always come from Him.

Heavenly Father, please help me to be a cheerful, generous giver. I want to share Your hope and love by helping provide for others' needs in Your name. I trust that You will always bless and provide for me too. Amen.

Day 339

NEWCOMERS

You and the Levites and the foreigners residing among you shall rejoice in all the good things the LORD your God has given to you and your household.

DEUTERONOMY 26:11 NIV

The Bible makes clear that our attitude toward strangers and newcomers must always be one of welcome and acceptance. In this verse, the Bible is telling us that we have more in common with these people than we may think. God has blessed all of us, and we can unite our hearts in gratitude. We don't need to be afraid that there won't be enough to go around, because God will supply. He will take care of our individual households—and as we trust Him to do that, we can lift our hearts in thanksgiving and generosity with those who are new to our communities. Thanksgiving is the antidote to fear and distrust.

Lord God, give me a grateful heart that isn't afraid to welcome newcomers.

WHOLE AND HEALTHY

When Jesus heard this, he told them, "Healthy people don't need a doctor—sick people do. I have come to call not those who think they are righteous, but those who know they are sinners."
MARK 2:17 NLT

With Jesus, we never need to pretend to be something we aren't. We don't need to impress Him with our spiritual maturity and mental acuity. Instead, we can come to Him honestly, with all our neediness, admitting just how weak we are. When we do, we let down the barriers that keep Him out of our hearts. We allow His grace to make us whole and healthy.

Jesus, help me to resist the temptation to be something I'm not. Instead, give me a spirit of vulnerability so that I can receive Your healing grace. Amen.

HOPE FROM THE HEROES

Faith shows the reality of what we hope for; it is the evidence of things we cannot see. Through their faith, the people in days of old earned a good reputation.
HEBREWS 11:1–2 NLT

Let Hebrews 11 strengthen you today. It defines what our faith is—being sure of what we hope for and certain of what we do not see—and gives us an incredible summary of so many heroes who've gone before us, holding to their faith. Their examples inspire us to keep on believing and being obedient to God, even when we can't see all of His plans or the final result. Think of how you'd like your name to be remembered among your family and friends and future generations as one who never gave up on God. Though we cannot see all that He is doing right now, we absolutely will one day soon.

Heavenly Father, please inspire me with renewed hope as I read about the heroes of the faith in Your Word. I want to persevere like they did. Amen.

SATISFIED

Satisfy us in the morning with your unfailing love,
that we may sing for joy and be glad all our days.
PSALM 90:14 NIV

God wants to fulfill you. He wants you to feel satisfied with life so that you will catch yourself humming or singing His praises all day long. Even when life is hard, He is waiting to comfort you with His unfailing love so that gladness will creep over your heart once more.

Father, You are the author of joy. Thank You so much for Your unfailing love that fills me to the brim. Give me grace and gladness every minute of every day. Amen.

RELATIONSHIP

My voice shalt thou hear in the morning, O LORD; in the morning will I direct my prayer unto thee, and will look up.
PSALM 5:3 KJV

Scheduling time to pray and read the Bible can feel like just another item on your to-do list. But getting to know God is not a project. It's a relationship. Best friends don't spend time together just because they feel they should. They do it because they enjoy each other's company and long to know each other better. The more consistent you are in spending time with God each day, the closer a friend you'll feel He is to you.

Jesus, I'm so amazed that I get to have a personal relationship with You! Plant a desire in my heart to seek You and hear from You every day of my life.

STRONGER TOGETHER

*I long to visit you so I can bring you some spiritual
gift that will help you grow strong in the Lord.
When we get together, I want to encourage you in your
faith, but I also want to be encouraged by yours.*

ROMANS 1:11–12 NLT

Think of your family and friends who also follow Jesus and
aren't afraid to show it. With great gratitude, focus on what
a blessing they are. We all need each other, and together we
make each other stronger. We spread hope and encouragement to one another by sharing the gifts we've received from
the Holy Spirit, by telling how God is working in our lives, by
praying for each other, and by reminding each other of the
truths of the Bible.

*Heavenly Father, thank You for the dear people in my
life who help make my faith in You stronger every day.
Help me to encourage and make them stronger too. Amen.*

DAILY MIRACLES

"That is why I tell you not to worry about everyday life—whether you have enough food and drink, or enough clothes to wear. Isn't life more than food, and your body more than clothing?"
MATTHEW 6:25 NLT

With our eyes fixed on what we don't have, we often overlook the grace we have already received. God has blessed us in many ways. Our bodies function day after day in amazing ways we take for granted, and life is filled with an abundance of daily miracles. Why do we worry so much about the details when we live in such a vast sea of daily grace?

Father, You are my provider. You have promised to give me everything I need. Help me to remember this truth and to lose myself in the vast sea of Your amazing grace. Amen.

THE PLANS OF THE LORD STAND FOREVER

The Lord brings the plans of nations to nothing.
He wrecks the plans of the people. The plans of the Lord
stand forever. The plans of His heart stand through the
future of all people. Happy is the nation whose God is the
Lord. Happy are the people He has chosen for His own.
PSALM 33:10–12 NLV

Worry and fear that others might have bad plans toward you can make you feel helpless and hopeless. So never forget that God wrecks the plans of the people if He wants to. He can wreck any malicious plan that someone might be plotting against you. And if He does allow something bad to happen to you, He has a greater plan for making you stronger because of it and turning it into something good instead. Romans 8:28 (NLV) promises, "God makes all things work together for the good of those who love Him and are chosen to be a part of His plan."

Heavenly Father, I believe You can wreck any bad plan
or turn it into good in the way that only You can do.
Your plans are always the best, and I trust You! Amen.

BECAUSE THE LORD IS YOUR SHEPHERD

The LORD is my shepherd, I lack nothing. He makes me lie down in green pastures, he leads me beside quiet waters, he refreshes my soul. He guides me along the right paths for his name's sake. Even though I walk through the darkest valley, I will fear no evil, for you are with me; your rod and your staff, they comfort me.
PSALM 23:1–4 NIV

The Lord God is your Shepherd leading you and giving you everything you need. Let the words of this well-known psalm infuse you with hope and strength and courage. Memorize it and repeat it throughout your day; let it encourage you in the midst of whatever you are facing!

Dear Lord, because You lead me and care for me, I have nothing to fear. Not one thing! Thank You, thank You, my loving Shepherd! Amen.

Day 348

PERCEPTION

*"The LORD himself goes before you and will be
with you; he will never leave you nor forsake you.
Do not be afraid; do not be discouraged."*
DEUTERONOMY 31:8 NIV

The world we see with our eyes is only a piece of reality, a
glimpse into an enormous and mysterious universe. Just as
our eyes often deceive us, so do our feelings. We perceive life
through our emotions, but they are as limited as our physical
vision. Whether we sense God's presence or not, He is always
with us. Grace waits to meet us in the future, so we can disre-
gard all our feelings of fear and discouragement.

*Father, even though I sometimes feel alone, You remind me
that my feelings are not facts, for You are always with me.
Thank You for the peace Your presence provides. Amen.*

Day 349

ENCOURAGING EACH OTHER

And let us not neglect our meeting together,
as some people do, but encourage one another.
HEBREWS 10:25 NLT

It's not always easy to practice gratitude. When things are going
"our way," we may find that gratitude comes more naturally
to us. But when everything seems to be going wrong, whether
our lives are falling apart in big ways or small irritations are
accumulating, then thanksgiving becomes harder to practice.
When we find ourselves struggling with gratitude, it's good to
be able to get encouragement from others. We don't have to
do life alone. In fact, the Bible tells us repeatedly that the spiritual life is healthier and easier when it's done in community.
So when gratitude becomes hard, lean on others—and then
allow others to lean on you when the shoe is on the other foot.

Thank You, Jesus, for Your body, the community of faith.
May I never separate myself from others who are following You.

EVERY STEP YOU TAKE

Let the Holy Spirit lead you in each step. Then you will not please your sinful old selves. The things our old selves want to do are against what the Holy Spirit wants. The Holy Spirit does not agree with what our sinful old selves want.
GALATIANS 5:16–17 NLV

Think of times when you've needed to be led in each step. Maybe on a really tough hike in the woods or mountains. Or maybe in physical therapy when recovering from an injury or surgery. Or maybe in navigating your way through grief. Really, though, think about how every day of your life you need to be led in each step to live a life that is pleasing to God. All on your own, you will do what your old sinful self wants. But with God's Holy Spirit in you, you can let Him lead you to do what He wants for you. And since He made you and loves you more than anyone else, you can trust that what He wants is always best for you!

Holy Spirit, please lead me in each step of my life. When I start to go my own way, please guide me back to You! I know what You want is always what's best. Amen.

QUESTIONS FOR JOB

"Where were you when I began building the earth? Tell Me, if you have understanding. Who decided how big it was to be, since you know? Who looked to see if it was as big as it should be? What was it built upon? Who laid its first stone, when the morning stars sang together and all the sons of God called out for joy? Who shut up the sea with doors, when it rushed out from its secret place?"

JOB 38:4–8 NLV

God asks Job some rhetorical questions that He knows Job knows the answers to. The questioning is a reminder to Job that God alone is all-knowing, all-powerful, amazing, and every other awesome adjective. There is only one true God who has extraordinary power to create and control all things. No matter what is feeling so hard and overwhelming in your life right now, you can have great hope in our almighty Creator God who is also your heavenly Father, your loving Savior, Jesus Christ, and the powerful Holy Spirit within you. Worship Him today and every day and trust Him with your life, because He alone is able to do absolutely anything!

Heavenly Father, You are the awesome answer to every question about who creates and has power and does all good things! I am so blessed to hope in You and worship You! Amen.

"EXTENDED" FAMILY

God sets the lonely in families.
PSALM 68:6 NIV

God knows that we need others. We need their love and support, their understanding, and their simple physical presence nearby. That is why He gives us families. Families don't need to be related by blood, though. They might be the people you work with, or the people you go to church with, or the group of friends you've known since grade school. Whoever they are, they're the people who make God's grace real to you every day.

Father, thank You for creating me with a longing for connection. Thank You for those You have placed in my life to make me more of who You created me to be. Amen.

Day 353

UNGRATEFULNESS

People will be lovers of themselves, lovers of money, boastful, proud, abusive, disobedient to their parents, ungrateful, unholy, without love, unforgiving, slanderous, without self-control, brutal, not lovers of the good, treacherous, rash, conceited, lovers of pleasure rather than lovers of God—having a form of godliness but denying its power.

2 TIMOTHY 3:2–5 NIV

The Bible rates the opposite of being thankful—being ungrateful—as just as dangerous as being selfish, greedy, gossipy, hateful, and abusive. People without gratitude may look godly and spiritual from the outside, but they lack the true inner power that the love of God gives to us. If we turn this verse around and look at the positive attributes, we see that being thankful goes along with being unselfish, generous, humble, gentle, respectful of parents, holy, loving, forgiving, kind, self-controlled, lovers of goodness, trustworthy, careful, and lovers of God. People like this have true spiritual power.

Lord, may my love for You be true, filled with gratitude and all the other virtues that go along with it.

DECISIONS, DECISIONS

*O my soul, thou hast said unto the Lord, Thou art
my Lord: my goodness extendeth not to thee.*
PSALM 16:2 KJV

Paper or plastic. Right or left. Yes or no. Every day is filled with
decisions that need to be made. Some have little bearing on the
big picture of our lives, while others can change its course in
dramatic ways. Inviting God into our decision-making process
is not only wise but helps us find peace with the decisions we
make. Knowing God is at work, weaving all our decisions into
a life of purpose, helps us move forward with confidence.

*I trust Your plan for my life, Lord. I invite You to
renew my mind and transform my thinking. I want
my thoughts and actions to be pleasing to You.*

PUT TO THE TEST

"For the Lord your God is putting you to the test to see if you love the Lord your God with all your heart and with all your soul. Follow the Lord your God and fear Him. Keep His Laws, and listen to His voice. Work for Him, and hold on to Him."

DEUTERONOMY 13:3–4 NLV

Don't let tests in life discourage you. Remember that God allows them at times to see if your faith in Him alone is real and if you love Him with all your heart and soul. These are tests you sure do want to pass with flying colors! So listen to God, obey Him, follow Him, and work for Him. Hold on tight to faith in the one true God, the only one worthy of faith, and watch how He reveals His faithfulness to you in return.

Heavenly Father, please help me to have hope even in the midst of difficult tests that prove how much I love You and believe in You. I never want to stop holding on to faith in You and You alone. Amen.

ON TRACK

Good and upright is the LORD:
therefore will he teach sinners in the way.
PSALM 25:8 KJV

When you're driving in an unfamiliar city, a map is an invaluable tool. It can help prevent you from taking wrong turns. If you do wind up headed in the wrong direction, a map can help set you back on track. God's Word and His Spirit are like a GPS for your life. Staying in close contact with God through prayer will help you navigate the best route to take in this life, one decision at a time.

Thank You for rerouting me when I take a wrong turn, Father. The end result is always You. When I can't find my way, You gently call me back to Your plans and purposes.

Day 357

FOLLOW JESUS

*"Whoever serves me must follow me;
and where I am, my servant also will be.
My Father will honor the one who serves me."*
John 12:26 niv

A disciple is someone who follows. That is the discipline
we practice: We follow Jesus. Wherever He is, we go. In His
presence, we find the daily grace we need to live. As we serve
Him, God honors us; He affirms our dignity and makes us all
we were meant to be.

*Jesus, I long to be Your disciple. Give me the grace
to follow You, a heart to serve You, and a mind in
tune with You every minute of every day. Amen.*

DAVID'S CONFIDENCE

But David said to Saul, ". . . Your servant has killed both
the lion and the bear. And this Philistine who has not gone
through our religious act will be like one of them. For he has
made fun of the armies of the living God." And David said,
"The Lord Who saved me from the foot of the lion and from the
foot of the bear, will save me from the hand of this Philistine."
Saul said to David, "Go, and may the Lord be with you."
1 SAMUEL 17:34, 36–37 NLV

David was sure he could fight the giant Goliath. He knew God
had helped him fight lions and bears in the past, and so God
would also help him fight the Philistine giant whom everyone else was afraid of. Let David's example encourage you.
Sometimes you simply need to remember all the ways God has
helped you fight and win in the past, and that act of remembrance can give you everything you need to let God help you
win whatever battle you need to fight right now.

Heavenly Father, when I face a battle, fill me with
hope and confidence by reminding me how You
have made me victorious in the past. Amen.

THE PROPER VANTAGE POINT

"My grace is all you need. My power works best in weakness." So now I am glad to boast about my weaknesses, so that the power of Christ can work through me.

2 Corinthians 12:9 nlt

So often, we feel as though we're not enough. Not smart enough, not talented enough, not popular enough, not attractive enough. . .the list can go on and on. But God reminds us that His grace is all we need. Where we are "not enough," He is more than enough! The word "boast" used in this verse meant, according to HELPS Word-studies, to "live with the head up high"; to "have the particular vantage point, the right base of operation, to deal successfully with a matter." Gratitude gives us the right vantage point. It allows God to make us strong through our weaknesses.

Help me, Lord Jesus, to see things from Your vantage point so that I may always boast in You.

Day 360

LOOK UP!

The heavens declare the glory of God;
the skies proclaim the work of his hands.
PSALM 19:1 NIV

Grace is as near as the sky over your head. Look up and be reminded of how wonderful God truly is. The same God who created the sun and the atmosphere, the stars and the galaxies, the same God who day by day creates a new sunrise and a new sunset, that same God loves you and creates beauty in your life each day!

Father, when I look to the heavens, I am reminded that You are Creator, giver of grace, and author of beauty. Thank You for surrounding me with the work of Your hands. Amen.

THE UNCHANGING ONE

"I am the LORD, and I do not change."
MALACHI 3:6 NLT

Some people love and thrive on variety and change in life, while others dread it. Change, especially sudden change, can make people feel hopeless and out of control. And so the peace and assurance that come from focusing on God's unchanging nature are especially refreshing and uplifting. "Jesus Christ is the same yesterday, today, and forever" (Hebrews 13:8 NLT). Nothing and no one else in all creation can make that claim. His "plans stand firm forever; his intentions can never be shaken" (Psalm 33:11 NLT). Moreover, "He never changes or casts a shifting shadow" (James 1:17 NLT).

Heavenly Father, when too much change makes me feel panicky and hopeless, help me to cling more tightly to Your unchanging, eternal nature. You are sovereign and good and in control of every detail of all Your perfect plans. Fill me with Your consistent, persistent peace. Amen.

DEEPEST LONGINGS

Lord, all my desire is before thee;
and my groaning is not hid from thee.
PSALM 38:9 KJV

What does your heart long for most? Talk to God about it.
He'll help you uncover the true root of your deepest desires.
Longing for a child? Perhaps what you're really longing for is
unconditional love. Longing for a home of your own? Perhaps
it's a need for security or to be admired by others that you
crave. Ultimately, God is the only one who can fill your deepest
longings—and it's His desire to do exactly that.

Father, I'm asking You to reveal to me the longings of
my heart. Show me the truths behind my desires, and
shine Your light where I need to see what I'm missing.

OVERPOWERING HOPE

We want you to know for sure about those who have died. You have no reason to have sorrow as those who have no hope. We believe that Jesus died and then came to life again. Because we believe this, we know that God will bring to life again all those who belong to Jesus.

1 THESSALONIANS 4:13–14 NLV

If you've experienced the loss of a family member or friend, you know the pain and sorrow can be excruciating. But even while you ache and grieve, you can have hope that overpowers the pain and sadness, because if your loved ones trusted Jesus, then they will be brought to life again just as He rose again. The promise of eternal life brings extraordinary, incredible comfort and hope—and it should motivate us to share the good news of Jesus with others. Just like God does, we should want all people to be saved from sin (1 Timothy 2:4).

Heavenly Father, remind me every moment of the hope of Jesus to overpower the pain of grief and loss. Help me to share the good news and help others to receive You as Savior so we all can be raised to life again with You forever. Amen.

AN INTIMATE RELATIONSHIP

"Oh, that we might know the LORD! Let us press on to know him. He will respond to us as surely as the arrival of dawn or the coming of rains in early spring."

HOSEA 6:3 NLT

We have the privilege of being in an intimate relationship with the Creator of the universe. That's an amazing fact! The more we yearn to know Him, the more He reaches out to us. The more we struggle to grow closer to Him, the more He helps us to do just that. Even when our hearts grow cold or full of doubt, He continues to work to bring us to Him. We can be so grateful that He longs for us even more than we long for Him. He is working moment by moment to draw us close to Him—and His love is as reliable as the sunrise, as dependable as spring rainfall.

Creator God, thank You that You love me and want to be my friend.

TRUST HIM TO MULTIPLY

Another of his disciples, Andrew, Simon Peter's brother, spoke up, "Here is a boy with five small barley loaves and two small fish, but how far will they go among so many?"
JOHN 6:8–9 NIV

"How far will they go among so many?" Jesus' disciple Andrew asked. We can relate when we wonder how our meager provisions or our finances or even our energy can possibly meet the great demands in our lives. With our human limits and weaknesses, we can feel utterly hopeless. But just as Jesus took five loaves and two fish to feed multitudes of people with loads left over, God is able to take anything we have and turn it into so much more to meet our needs and the needs of others. Offer Him everything you have, and then trust Him to multiply it in miraculous ways.

Dear Jesus, remind me that You can take my smallest offering to You and turn it into far, far above and beyond what I need and hope for. I praise and thank You! Amen.

SCRIPTURE INDEX

OLD TESTAMENT

NEW TESTAMENT

YOU ARE IMPORTANT TO GOD
. . .AND DEEPLY LOVED!

The Self-Care Devotional

Better than a bubble bath. . .more rejuvenating than an
expensive spa treatment. . .these 180 calming, comforting
devotions and prayers are just the nourishment your weary
soul needs to rest and recharge. Six months of daily readings
touch on topics important to you, including Understanding
Your Feelings, Protecting Your Schedule, Nourishing Your
Soul, Finding Joy, Shining Your Light, Pressing Pause,
Making Time for Rest, and Being Kind to Yourself.

Flexible Casebound / 978-1-63609-749-7

DAILY INSPIRATION FOR A WOMAN'S SPIRIT!

365 Devotional Prayers for Women

This daily devotional prayer book is a lovely reminder to bring any petition before your heavenly Father. Hundreds of just-right-sized prayers touch on topics that will help you grow a courageous faith.

DiCarta / 978-1-63609-744-2

Daily Devotions to Nurture Your Faith

This beautiful daily devotional collection will engage your spirit with Bible wisdom and encouraging devotions. Each entry includes a scripture, faith-nurturing devotional reading, and prayer.

DiCarta / 978-1-63609-722-0